A TIME TO BUILD

THE CUPBEARER'S STRATEGY

ATSEN JONATHAN AHUA

 www.trafford.com

North America & international
toll-free: 1 888 232 4444 (USA & Canada)
fax: 812 355 4082

Dedicated to my patient spouse of three decades and more, Liz Kpam Ahua and all those who strive in the most challenging of circumstances to do what is right because it is the right thing to do, the Nehemiahs of our generation and the next.

ACKNOWLEDGEMENTS

I am grateful to my primary 1 teacher at the Mkar Demonstration School, Elder Moor Kpire of blessed memory who penned the name Nehemiah with indelible ink on my young mind. The way he pronounced it was unforgettable. It gave you the impression of a formidable force landing with permanence and finality.

His son, my friend of many decades, Nehemiah Ayila Moor kept the memory alive by reminding me time and again that he did not like how the name sounded like a heavy blow.

However, it was Dr. Dela Adadevoh of Campus Crusade for Christ who really fired my imagination with the character of Nehemiah and his relevance to our times with his exposition on the cupbearer and his leadership qualities.

I acknowledge them and the many other individuals and groups in the African Diaspora and the homeland that have provided the backdrop against which to view and model the cupbearer's strategy for reconstruction. Thanks to Benue artists Dan Nyikwagh and Joe Awuhe for the illustrations and portraits and to computer whizz, Torrumun Atii for assistance with the graphics.

CONTENTS

TIME

Forced Slavery, Voluntary Slavery

There was a time when able-bodied young men and women were captured and taken from the West Coast of Africa, transported against their will and desire to work as slaves in distant lands to be the wealth and to create the wealth of others. Four centuries down the line, able-bodied and intelligent young men and women mainly from West Africa, and increasingly from the eastern side of the continent uproot themselves, burn their bridges, beg, borrow and steal to go to foreign lands where they will work at menial jobs.

An uncomfortably large number do not make it. Some are claimed by the harsh Sahara desert against which they pit themselves in a desperate unequal struggle. Others are lost in the depths of the Mediterranean when the thoroughly unsafe small boats in which they seek to cross the sea to the shores of Europe capsize and dump them in the water instead. In the later years of the Gadhafi regime, a macabre chapter was added to the saga with the capture and execution of scores of West Africans found to have entered Libya illegally in their quest to cross over to Europe. In the heady days of the dream to end all problems of the terrestrial ball by the year 2000, that magical year seemed so far away. Even as the days closed in upon us and the deadlines that we had set ourselves for the year 2000 receded farther and farther into the distant horizon, we clung on with hope.

The reality has proved that the dire straits have multiplied and the level of desperation increased phenomenally.

". . . a boat carrying an estimated 200 migrants capsized off the Sicilian island of Lampedusa Friday, October 11, 2013. The capsizing occurred some 65 miles (105 kilometres) south-east of Lampedusa, but in waters where Malta has search and rescue responsibilities. Last week, a boat carrying some 500 Eritreans capsized off Lampedusa, killing at least 339. Only 155 people survived."

Eritrea is an eastern African country occupying an area of 121,320 square kilometers (46,841 square miles and a population of slightly over 6 million inhabitants. It borders Sudan to the north and west, Ethiopia and Djibouti to the south, and the Red Sea to the east. Its land borders extend for 1,630 kilometers (1,012 miles), while its total coastline is 2,234 kilometers (1,388 miles). Eritrea's capital, Asmara, and its 2 other major cities, Assab and Massawa, are in the southeastern and eastern parts of the country. The country emerged as an independent state after decades of a grueling war with Ethiopia. The war was won when the freedom fighters of Eritrea joined forces with the dissidents fighting to overthrow the communist regime of the dictator Mengitsu Haile Mariam.

The military dictator who had himself overthrown the Octogenarian Emperor Haile Selassie, a descendant of the ancient Abyssinian military dynasties had embraced communism with ardent passion and put down the boot on his ancient people with brutal ferocity. Nobody was sorry to see him go and very few mourned him when he died in exile in Zimbabwe, Southern Africa in April 2013.

Having overcome their common enemy and achieved their territorial ambitions, the two partners in the fight for freedom, Meles Zenawi of Ethiopia and Esias Afeworki of Eritrea then turned on each other and started slugging it out with tenacious ferocity. Twenty years after its independence from Ethiopia and several clashes down the road, Eritrea and Ethiopia are still officially at war.

The two countries have stayed at daggers drawn because of territorial disputes and the unwillingness of the parties to negotiate a conclusive peace or accept the verdict of international mediating bodies. Consequently, between 1998 and 2012, several pitched battles have been fought and much blood spilled over a patch of land that may not be large enough to contain the graves of the dead in the fratricidal battles that have wracked the fragile resources of the two countries. Estimates of the number of casualties on both sides in these battles range between 70,000 and 300,000, a large number of citizens to be lost by any country.

The reality on the ground is that the second youngest state in Africa is in a perpetual state of war. The war of independence was just the beginning. No one sees the prospect for peace under the leadership of its independent-minded and mercurial leader, Isaias Afewerki. President Afewerki has been holding tightly onto the reins of power since his victorious fighters took control of Eritrean territory from the Red Sea in the East to Gash Barka on the border with Sudan to the West.

The consequences of Eritrea's warlike stance are that every young man and young woman for that matter is an automatic military conscript. No man, below the age of 54 is exempt from military service. No woman below the age of 40 is exempt unless she is married with children.

If you are an able-bodied Eritrean, you have to do your duty to bear arms and be prepared to pay the supreme sacrifice to the nation. As an Eritrean man, you are not allowed to travel outside the country if you are below the age of 54, except with express presidential permission. The same applies to a woman if you are below the age of 40.

Fleeing from military conscription in their iron-clad country with the certainty of capital punishment hanging over their heads, the young people of Eritrea have a good idea of what possible fate awaits them in the Red Sea, the Sahara Desert or the Mediterranean if they succeed in getting that far. If there is any shred of hope, they will take the chance.

For any nation to lose more than 300 of its young men and all the potential in them in one fell swoop, pitting themselves against the elements on a journey that should never have been embarked upon, in an accident that should never have happened is sad. It is very sad. But this fact does not deter others from trying.

Hope springs eternal in the human spirit.

How else does one explain the fact that in less than a week after the perishing of the 339 Eritrean youth near Lampedusa, another boat on the same mission sinks in the same area with its own cargo of hopeful migrants? The boat capsizes and scores die but a few scores get through. And for some of those fished out with life in them, their broad smiles and victory signs, in spite of the hell they have come through show that in their minds, they have arrived and achieved their objectives.

For others the stories are even more chilling. In their desperate overland journeys across Sudan and Egypt to the Mediterranean some become victims of the purveyors of the illegal and immoral trade in human organs and body parts. They end up as unwilling donors of kidneys, livers, lungs and hearts and any other organ that the body part harvesters can find use for. Harrowing as these stories are, they do not discourage others from trying.

There are those who arrive on some European shore against all the odds. The majority of these will of course end up in some detention centre to spend years and years of their lives in the hope of getting an asylum status that could enable them to integrate into the society and economy of the country of their desperate dreams.

A miniscule number from this desperate group may get through all the hoops. There are those who, undocumented, live as non-persons that for all practical purposes do not exist. They may die undocumented and nobody back home will be any the wiser. Some as illegal aliens live a precarious life on the periphery of the periphery of society.

The many trouble spots of Africa continue to spew out more of the displaced and dispossessed. The economies of countries struggling with the fundamentals of nation building reel under mounting pressures from within and without. Social systems disrupted by conflicts and the devaluation of human life continue to add to the numbers of the displaced and dispossessed including the trafficked around the world.

The portion of the world endowed with wealth and power applies palliatives to the sores of the continent and closes its gates against hordes of the desperate poor scrambling for its endowments. So the young people, and some not so young, continue to risk all in the search for a foothold in the foreign lands of promise. The lure of the foreign Eldorado is so powerful in the rich poor countries of Africa that for some young and not so young adventurers, the idea of getting out conjures images of prosperous Utopia on the other side.

Angst of the Diaspora

Those with the experience know better. There are those who succeed in establishing themselves in these foreign lands. They carry the passports of some North American or European country. They are the citizens of these adopted lands but mostly far from satisfied. They may enjoy the running water, the good public transport system, credit cards and other basic comforts and conveniences of life that are offered by the industrialized world. Some may even make enough money to pay the bills and establish a comfort zone for themselves and their immediate families.

But even a casual discussion reveals that their hearts are still very much with the lands of their birth. When you scratch a little deeper, you find the pervasive feeling of discontent.

There are those who will come out and tell you that no matter how hard they try, they can at best aspire to second-class citizenship in these countries. There is the pervasive wish that things were better organized to provide opportunities for them to realize their full potential in Africa, the continent of their birth.

Yet there are those who feel bitterness towards Africa; who are painfully aware of the complicity of their African kith and kin in the enslavement of their ancestors or their unwilling exile. They are conscious of those who grew wealthy from trading in the blood and flesh of their ancestors and cut them off from their roots.

There are those whose bitterness is steeped in the pangs of betrayal, the reality of being hunted by intolerant governments or chased out of their homes by purveyors of conflict, forced to submerge their dignity in the humbling and sometimes degrading waters of asylum seeking and refugee status in foreign lands.

There are those who feel the need and a strong motivation to make a contribution towards change for the better in the land of their origins but they do not know from where to start. Let us reflect together. Perhaps we will find a way.

MODELS FROM THE NEAR EAST

Some of the peoples of the Middle East with which Africa has been in contact for a few thousand years have the advantage of millennia of recorded history. Their history, legend and heroic writings are replete with larger than life characters as well as true to life ones. Their stories give us some examples and lessons in leadership and community building. Their stories tell of times of upbeat nationalistic fervour and prosperity and times of descent into the nadir of despair followed by recovery and regeneration.

A Man Called Nehemiah

As I reflect on my various discussions with Africans in the Diaspora, the story of one of these characters keeps coming to mind. He was a Jewish captive in exile in the court of the Emperor Artaxerxes Longimanus of the Persian Empire and his name was Nehemiah. His memoirs, which are included as the 16th book in the Christian holy book of books the Bible, reveal a man with remarkable strategic vision and outstanding qualities of leadership.

He comes across as impassioned in speech and prayer, faithful in his trust in God and highly capable as an organizer. His single-minded resolve and focus on the task at hand, his quick and decisive response to problems and his unselfishness are some of the qualities that mark him out as a model worthy of examination and possible emulation.

Nehemiah occupied a position of confidentiality and trust as cupbearer to the emperor Artaxerxes. Authoritative commentators tell us that a cupbearer was an officer of considerable importance in the courts of Middle Eastern monarchs of the time. The holder of this office was brought into confidential relations with the monarch and had to be thoroughly trust-worthy, as part of his duty was to guard against poison in the king's cup. In some cases he was required to taste the wine before presenting it.

Nehemiah was therefore quite comfortable in the court of Artaxerxes and could have lived his life enjoying the largesse that his position brought him in the empire without a headache. He could have perhaps been looking forward to a comfortable retirement with a sizeable nest egg consisting of lucrative Persian stocks and options for his old age. Nehemiah set out to build a wall around his beloved home city of Jerusalem. His objective was to provide security for his people that had returned from exile and started the reconstruction of the temple of their God and their devastated towns and villages. He ended up providing one of the most enduring lessons in leadership and the blueprint for a reconstruction strategy.

My Locus Standi

But what is my locus standi for even having the audacity and the ogaligancy (don't look for that word in the dictionary) to dare to raise such a subject? As my Nigerian siblings may ask, "Na who send you sef?" I lay no claim to any special knowledge but for the privilege of a variegated life experience. I crave your indulgence. If you can rustle up the patience to give me a moment or two of your precious time, I will explain.

Ndoghur Kpoo to Atemityo

In my first decade on earth, I survived the ***Ndoghur Kpoo,*** the hacking cough that cut down the young, the men and women in their prime and the old without fear or favour in the 1950s and 1960s. Some of my mates were not so lucky.

Later in life I learnt that it was a man-made disease, born of the French nuclear weapons tests in the Sahara desert and borne on the wings of the powerful Harmattan winds that seasonally muscled their way from the North African desert across the Niger-Benue valley, pushing the inter-tropical convergence zone to the edge of the mangrove swamp forest of the Niger delta.

In 1961, I survived the ***nande-nande,*** the self-inflicted spate of hate-induced arson unleashed by brother against brother and sister courtesy of the machinations of politicians bent on manipulating the trust and enthusiasm of their simple followers for the satisfaction of their selfish dreams of grandeur or simply to horn their megalomaniac skills for the next level of horse-trading in bellicosity.

In 1964, I survived ***atemityo,*** the pervasive bloodletting among my beloved Tiv siblings spurred on by a hateful naivety that did not make sense to my twelve-year-old mind. Yes, I saw the body of a dear 'Uncle', mutilated with machete chops and left in the rain for 4 days, blown to 4 times its size and oozing stench and goo because he supposedly associated with 'them' instead of 'us'. It had become increasingly difficult to distinguish between what constituted the 'them' and what the 'us'.

As I enter my seventh decade of life with the benefit of intercourse across four continents and the entire colour spectrum of humanity, I still find difficulty with defining that elusive them and us.

In that same year of the ***atemityo***, I sat on a wooden bench across a crude table from the legendary Tondo Agede, he whose magical machete had separated so many hapless heads of the hated **Baja** from their bodies. I stared with childish fascination at the small inconsequential-looking man in a dirty **danshiki** while he wolfed down the meal of pounded yam and spring chicken basted in brown melon seed dough spiced with locust-bean seed and black pepper sauce that my mother had specially prepared for him. As I hoped in my childish curiosity that he would do one of those magical things that I had heard so often about him, my father was busy pleading with him, as it turned out in vain, to let go of his career of bloodshed and give his life to Jesus Christ.

My father was an evangelist from the second wave of Christian converts in Tivland who had never looked back since his conversion to Christianity in the mid-1930s.

In 1966, as I entered my mid-teens, the polarization between them and us culminated in a coup *d'état* that snowballed into a three-year long civil war. In that year, I had moved out for the first time into a community of those who spoke languages other than my Tiv mother-tongue and began to broaden my horizon. I happily mingled with youth from other parts of Nigeria in the Christian boarding school ran by American missionaries mainly from Michigan State. At W. M. Bristow Secondary located in Gboko in the heartland of the Benue valley, we were all made to feel as members of a cohesive community with the shared value of being the "light of the world". We proudly wore our school motto emblazoned in Latin on the school badge that made up the breast pocket of the white shirt of our school uniform: *"Vos Estis Lux Mundi"*

It was painful and confusing when our school mates from the Ibo-speaking region of the country suddenly and quietly disappeared from among us. It was frustrating and incomprehensible to our young minds that our friends who had nothing to do with whatever was the issue between the leaders who were at daggers drawn with one another should become victims of the conflict, their education broken and their lives disrupted.

From the Backwater to the Largest Safe

In the 1970s, by the grace of God and my own discipline, I moved from the backwater villages of the Benue valley to acquire an education that led to my exposure to the width and depth of Nigeria and its diverse and dynamic people. Through the weather-beaten halls of Kings College Lagos that oozed privileged upbringing and the imposing concrete slabs of the University of Lagos I learnt a few things. There were Kwaggas from the Northeast and Dakarkaris from the Northwest that were neither Hausa nor Fulani. There were Eguns in the Southwest that were not Yoruba and Andonis in the Southeast that were not Ibo. I learnt with a combination of pride and bewilderment from the handbook of Nigerian languages that my country spoke some 396 languages. I was ready to embrace them all in the happy realization that talent and stupidity were not restricted to any particular tribe or tongue. I chose a career in media and communications that enabled me in the 1980s and 1990s to dance on the African stage and interact with my siblings of the West, the East, the North and the South. I have witnessed moments of elation in history and contributed in small ways to some. Through my association with the mass media, I have been a fly on the wall to witness dumb-founded as supposedly great men plotted with cunning and greed, the satiation of their appetites and supposedly small men show nobility of heart and mind only associated with the divine.

I have travelled across the five continents and interacted with humanity in its mind-boggling diversity and uniformity. I have lived in Africa outside Nigeria, the country of my birth since 1990 and for several years, almost against my personal will and desire, in the heart of Europe, the small land-locked, mountainous and terribly important country of Switzerland that dare not sneeze.

Of course everyone knows that as owner of the world's largest safe for the wealth of the world, Switzerland dare not sneeze if the whole world is to avoid coming down with a raging flu, bird, swine or whatever.

My Nigerian accent, coloured to some extent by my American teachers was firmly entrenched before I ventured out of my country first to East Africa and then to Europe. I don't think I am likely to live overseas long enough to acquire a foreign accent. I am yet to touch the assumed prosperity of the Diaspora. I can still see with the eyes of Africa. But I think I can also appreciate the hopes and frustrations of my Diaspora siblings and I can identify with their desires.

Of Grey Hair and Deja Vu

And now that my chronological age has crossed the half-century mark by more than ten years, and tufts of grey have started sprouting on my head, in my nostrils, my beard and even some unspeakable parts of my anatomy, the weight of fifty years of memories, and deja vu is beginning to tell. But even weightier is the push of dreams yet to be realized, obstacles yet to be scaled and walls to be built or broken down. I think this combination gives me the locus standi.

The Indian Guru, Shrishri Ravi Shankar, the founder and leader of the Art of Living Foundation postulates in one of his intimate notes to the sincere seeker: "The first sign of intelligence is to do nothing. The second is to ensure that whatever you have started, you finish it." I started writing this and I had to finish it. I know you are an intelligent person. Since you started reading this and have come this far, you owe it to yourself to go along with me and finish what you started.

Although the memoirs of Nehemiah are found in the Christian holy book, the Bible, its lessons are relevant to all humanity and at this time particularly to Africans of the Diaspora. I urge you to follow the story with me and perhaps you may find your place in the lessons that it unfolds.

THE STORY IN BRIEF

The memoirs of Nehemiah span a period of about 15 years in the 5th Century BC. I will not try to summarise the cupbearer's story. He tells it well himself with clarity and economy of words with a little help from Tyndale[1].

"In December of the 20th year of the reign of King Artaxerxes of Persia, when I was at the palace in Shushan, one of my fellow Jews named Hanani came to visit me with some men who had arrived from Judah. I took the opportunity to inquire about how things were going in Jerusalem. 'How are the Jews who returned to Jerusalem from their exile here getting along?' I asked.

'Well,' they replied, 'things are not good at all. The wall of Jerusalem is still torn down, and the gates still burned out.'

When I heard this, I sat down and cried. In fact I refused to eat for several days, for I spent the time in prayer to the God of heaven. One day in April four months later, as I was serving the king his wine, he asked me, 'Why so sad? You aren't sick are you? You

---

[1]   The verbatim quotations from the Book of Nehemiah are taken from The Living Bible Red Letter Large Print Edition published by Tyndale.

look like a man with deep troubles.' Until then I had always been cheerful when I was with him.

I was badly frightened but I replied, 'Let the king live forever. How can I not be sad? For the city where my ancestors are buried is in ruins and the gates have been burned down.' 'Well, what should be done?' the king asked. With a quick prayer to the God of heaven, I replied, 'If it please Your Majesty and if you look upon me with your royal favour, send me to Judah to rebuild the city of my fathers. The king replied with the queen seated beside him, 'How long will you be gone? When will you return?' So it was agreed and I set the time for my departure. Then I added to my request: 'If it please the king, give me letters to the governors west of the Euphrates River instructing them to let me travel through their countries on my way to Judah; also a letter to Asaph, the manager of the king's forest, instructing him to give me timber for the beams and for the gates of the fortress near the temple, and for the city walls and for a house for myself.' And the king granted these requests for God was being gracious to me."

MEMOIRS OF A CUP-BEARER

In examining the memoirs of Nehemiah and the role that he played in the reconstruction of Jerusalem and the restoration of his people, I notice that the empire that had been the source of the devastation of Judah and Jerusalem was also the source of the resources and authority that he used for the reconstruction of the city. I also notice the passion and concern of Nehemiah for a city and country that he could hardly have known at first hand. Nehemiah was probably born in exile and had never set eyes on Jerusalem but his passion for the city was such that when he learnt things were bad there, he developed what in today's parlance would be described as acute depression. He was acutely aware no doubt that as long as the city of his fathers was in ruins and exposed to security and adulteration hazards, he could never be at rest. He was aware that his fate in grand Persia was inextricably tied up with that of the people of Judah and the city of Jerusalem.

The second point that strikes me at this early stage of the memoirs is the readiness with which Nehemiah staked his career and his future on his commitment to the welfare of his people; these people whom he could hardly be said to have any first-hand knowledge of and who were the residents of some remote province far removed from the grandiose environment of the imperial court of Artaxerxes of Persia, noted for its pomp and pageantry in history.

In the second digital decade of the third millennium, we are no longer constrained by the physical distances that divided the Judean provinces from the imperial courts of Persia. The more of the terrestrial ball and its environment we explore, the more we realize the interconnected nature of all that is life and the environment of the cosmos. The more we get to learn that the most miniscule of the forms of life that we have on earth has the capacity to influence the momentous things on earth, the more we become conscious of the visible and invisible ties that bind us humans in our quest for a healthy, happy and prosperous life on earth.

Today, we realize that a colony of termites breaking the wind in a Cameroonian forest has significant impact on greenhouse gas emissions. In fact, the more we learn of our interconnectedness, the more we must realize that what happens in the forests of Central African Republic or the jungles of the Democratic Republic of Congo impacts on us whether we live in Oslo Norway, London in the United Kingdom or New York, USA. The cup-bearer continues his story. The problem is plain for everybody to see. The broken walls of Jerusalem and the gates burned with fire are in plain sight for all to see but it takes a Nehemiah to develop the vision of what to do and the strategy as to how to go about it.

Lessons in Reconnaissance

"Three days after I arrived at Jerusalem, I stole out during the night, taking a few men with me; for I hadn't told a soul about the plans for Jerusalem which God had put into my heart. I was mounted on my donkey and the others were on foot. And we went out through the Valley Gate toward the Jackal's well and over the Dung Gate to see the broken wall and burned gates. Then we went to the Fountain Gate and the King's Pool, but my donkey could not get through the rubble. So we circled the city, and I followed the brook, inspecting the wall, and entered again at the Valley Gate. The city officials did not know I had been out there, or why, for as yet I had said nothing to anyone about my plans—not the political or religious leaders, or even those who would be doing the work."

There is an important lesson in the prudence with which Nehemiah approached his task. He took three days to get an orientation to his environment and then under cover of night, carried out a thorough reconnaissance of the work he would be engaging himself and others in. Here is a man who had the support of the highest authority in the empire for the assignment that he was in the province to carry out. He also had a contingent of the military assigned by the Emperor himself to protect him. However, he did not charge into the fray on his white horse waving his instrument of authority and whipping everyone into line. He studied the situation in absolute discretion during which time he also formulated his strategy for mobilizing the people to the work. As events unfold, we see why his prudence was necessary. In his own words again.

'But when Sanballat the Horonite and Tobiah, an Ammonite who was a government official heard of my arrival, they were very angry that anyone was interested in helping Israel.'

The Horonite, the Ammonite and the Market for Evil

A considerable part of Nehemiah's memoirs concerns itself with the challenges that the duo of Sanballat the Horonite and Tobiah the Ammonite, occasionally supported by their friend Geshem the Arab pose to his agenda and his work. These characters are typical of the challenges that we are likely to encounter in our zealous and well-meaning efforts to contribute to the reconstruction of our various broken walls in Africa. Their nature, motivation, characters and tactics are worth examining in some detail as they pose one of the greatest challenges to successful human endeavour.

The sages tell an allegory of a certain worker of iniquity who went to the market of the devils to find more lethal weapons to replenish his arsenal of wickedness. He started by window-shopping and was impressed by the assortment of weapons of the flesh, of the mind and the spirit on display in the various pavilions of evil. The sexual ones were the most pervasive and relatively cheap. The ones that preyed on greed, violence and other negative emotions were also cheap and abundant. As the gentleman strolled around the market, he could not help noticing that a certain innocuous-looking weapon was given pride of place in every shop. Framed in a corner and carrying an astronomical price, it seemed to beckon with impudence to the shopper 'Come on! Give me a try!' Our worker of iniquity approached a young shopkeeper.

The young demon looked at our friend with admiration for his good taste in evil. "The master handles that one personally," he said. And sure enough the devil himself materialized right on cue full of guffaws.

"Hey Hey Hey my terrible friend; I admire your taste in evil. Now that you have attracted my personal attention, there's no doubt you will go far in evil. That, *Mon ami*, is what we call the *Nakamamatay armas ng Diacouragement*, in other words, the lethal weapon of discouragement. With it we have brought down the high and mighty, the lofty and the hefty. We unleash it innocuously. It penetrates the toughest hide insidiously and brings its victims down automatically. Once we unleash it, we don't have to do a thing more."

The Weapon of Discouragement

Nehemiah had to contend with discouragement many times during the project and so will you when you embark on any good work that seeks to improve the welfare of those less fortunate than you. This is a spiritual reality that we face in the gross material plane of this life in the struggle between good and evil. In Nehemiah's case, Sanballat the Horonite and his gang that was determined to stop him from rebuilding the walls of Jerusalem wielded the instrument of discouragement.

When I discuss with men and women of the African Diaspora from different backgrounds, I find invariably that God has put a certain desire in their hearts to make some sort of contribution to Africa. There is a broken wall and a burnt gate that gives them sleepless nights and makes them to go without food at times. For some, that wall has not been defined with the clarity that Nehemiah saw the Jerusalem wall and could respond without hesitation to the king: 'Give me a chance and resources and safe passage to go and rebuild the city of my ancestors.'

For some, the instrument of discouragement completes its task with them at this very first stage of even visualizing the problem. For some, the problems of Africa are so immense and so pervasive that they cannot see any concrete thing that they could possibly do to make a difference.

It is necessary to go beyond this first stage and identify your Jerusalem wall. If you look carefully enough, you might discover that your role consists of building a particular segment of the wall in collaboration with others who are like-minded and ready to be mobilized.

But we must beware of the Horonite and his weapon of discouragement. For you will surely find your own Horonite. So the first question you may ask is: 'In this good work that I want to do for the land of my ancestors, who is the Horonite with whom I have to contend?' As we continue with the memoirs of Nehemiah, it will become obvious what you should look out for in defining the Horonite lined up against your project.

Let us rebuild the Wall

After he had done his secret reconnaissance and returned to base, Nehemiah called the people and told them why he had come and what he had in mind. The reaction of Sanballat and his gang will give you an idea of how you can identify your Horonite. For you will tell the Horonite by his motivation, his agenda, his character and his tactics. Let us continue with the story according to Nehemiah's memoirs. He is now ready to reveal his agenda and his plan to his people.

"Now I told them 'you know full well the tragedy of our city, it lies in ruins and its gates are burnt. Let us rebuild the wall of Jerusalem and rid ourselves of this disgrace!' Then I told them about the desire God had put into my heart, and of my conversation with the king, and the plan to which he had agreed.

They replied at once, 'Good! Let us rebuild the wall!' And so the work began.

But when Sanballat and Tobiah and Geshem the Arab heard of our plan, they scoffed and said, 'What are you doing, rebelling against the king like this?' But I replied, 'The God of heaven will help us, and we his servants, will rebuild this wall; but you may have no part in this affair.' Then Eliashib the High Priest and the other priests rebuilt the wall as far as the tower of the hundred and the tower of Hananel; then they rebuilt the Sheep Gate, hung its doors and dedicated it.

Sanballat was very angry when he learnt that we were rebuilding the wall. He flew into a rage, and insulted and mocked us and laughed at us, and so did his friends and the Samaritan army officers. 'What does this bunch of poor, feeble Jews think they are doing?' he scoffed. Do they think they can build the wall in a day if they offer enough sacrifices? And look at those charred stones they are pulling out of the rubbish and using again!'

Tobiah who was standing beside him remarked, 'If even a fox walked along the top of their wall, it would collapse!'

Nature of the Horonite

From what we have learnt of the Horonite so far, it is obvious that his motivation is hatred and his orientation negative. Even the name of the Horonite is calculated to intimidate and perplex you and give you horrors in the night. The words of the Horonite and his conversation give an indication of his orientation and tactics. As his character unfolds, we see that he uses lies and falsehood, cunning and trickery, mockery and thuggery. So who is the Horonite lined up against you?

The agenda of the Horonite is a flexible one that is nevertheless focused on his principal objective that is to stop you. As we proceed with the story, we see that the Horonite will try to discourage you. If he fails in that respect, he will try to change your agenda to conform to his own and thereby to contain you. Sanballat sought first of all to discourage Nehemiah and his workers through insinuations and veiled threats. He accused them of putting up the wall in rebellion to the king.

Of course he had no idea that Nehemiah was there with the full approval and backing of the king. As a local politician, he probably had no inkling of the functioning of the empire, but here he was preening and pretending to be a protector of the interest of the king and Nehemiah was not the one to deflate his balloon either.

How would you have reacted if you were in Nehemiah's shoes? I would have probably whipped out my letter of authority from the king himself and ordered the soldiers in my entourage to frog-march Sanballat and his cohorts off my premises. Nehemiah politely informed Sanballat and his friends that he was doing God's work and really it was none of their business.

"Then I prayed, 'Hear us O Lord God, for we are being mocked. May their scoffing fall back upon their own heads, and may they themselves become captives in a foreign land! Do not ignore their sin. Do not blot it out, for they have despised you in despising us who are building your wall.'

Nehemiah saw the significance of the work he was doing beyond himself. It was not a personal ego trip to show his power and influence. It was not a test of strength between him and the local politicians. It was the work of God so its import was both great and good and he could afford not to join issues with the Horonite and his gang. That is why he prayed and continued working. It seems to me that if you are to identify a good work worth doing or a wall to build, it must be anchored in greatness and goodness. The cupbearer continues.

'At last the wall was completed to half its original height around the entire city—for the workers worked hard. But when Sanballat and Tobiah and the Arabians, Ammonites and Ashdodites heard that the work was going right ahead and that the breaks in the wall were being repaired, they became furious. They plotted to lead an army against Jerusalem to bring about riots and confusion. But we prayed to our God and guarded the city day and night to protect ourselves."

From jeering, laughter and mockery, we see the Horonite transforming his tactics from insinuations through lies and falsehood to open plots and threats of violence. Not only are his hatred and anger intensified but also he has broadened his circle of negativity to include the Ashdodites in addition to the Ammonites, the Arabians and the Horonites. After all, they had jeered that all it required was for a fox to walk on top of the reconstructed wall for it to collapse. Why not wait for the fox to collapse the wall? Why the need to mobilize an army to attack Jerusalem and create riots and confusion? But that is the nature of the Horonite.

The more you succeed in implementing the good work that you have chosen to do, the more furious you will make him and the more the opposition he will mobilize against you. The reference to the charred stones from the rubbish that the workers are pulling out to use in reconstructing the wall carries a potent imagery for those that will commit to the reconstruction of their fatherland. You will find that the material you have to work with will not be clean. In fact you will have to recycle people and resources that are charred and tainted and capable of being taunted and ridiculed. You may also be given a label as Nehemiah and his workers were tagged a 'bunch of poor feeble Jews'.

Charred Stones

You may also want to distinguish between a charred stone that is lying on the rubbish heap and one that has been selected and integrated into a construction project. A charred stone on its own lying on a rubbish heap hardly has any identity or role apart from constituting part of an eyesore. Once that stone has been selected, shaped and used as part of a construction project, its whole identity changes. It has an address and a definite role to play in a wall, or a foundation or a floor. So is it with humans. For some, without the selection and motivation of a Nehemiah, they will remain charred and blackened on the rubbish heap.

Three years ago, I was attending a funeral in the mountainside village of Mkar, some six and a half kilometres from my local government headquarters of Gboko. Mkar evokes so many memories in my head and feelings in my heart. It is the place where the South African missionaries who brought the message of salvation to Tivland with all its trappings of racial superiority and good-natured apartheid had set up shop way back in the first quarter of the 20th Century.

It is the village in which I had my primary education in the opening years of the 60s decade. It was in this village that I experienced for the first time that tingling feeling that courses through your being from the tips of your hair to the soles of your feet and sets your heart beating at breakneck speed. Yes, it was in this village that I experienced for the first time that feeling towards another being that a child is said to have describes as "an itch around the heart that you can't scratch". It was also in this village that my self-esteem suffered some of its toughest blows of childhood. So the village has lots of memories for me. At this funeral, another one was made.

Jack was a man I had admired and respected in all my impressionable years. In the absence of a polished and cultivated uncle in my immediate family circle, Jack was my uncle after whom I tried to model my bearing. At this funeral, I spied him in a group of other retired civil servants. He looked a pale shadow of the Jack I had known and admired. Threadbare and faded clothes worn with a degree of carelessness I would never have associated with him. It was not just age. Something had crumbled up inside Jack. He must have sensed my horror immediately.

As soon as he could, he detached himself form the group. He took me aside and said matter-of-factly: "I know what you are thinking. 'What a waste?' And I agree with you. Here I am at a time when I should be contributing the benefit of my experience and lessons learnt towards the development of our society but I am out on the shelf wasting away.

You know how I worked my ass off as chief economist and permanent secretary when we started this state from the scratch. Even if there were anything to steal, the thought would never have crossed our minds. I am talking about those of us who were trained to serve the people with integrity and dignity and tried our best so to do. We approached the job with idealism in our hearts and enthusiasm in our minds. We were kicked out ignominiously and the doors to further development have been banged in our faces. We cannot play the games of arrant dishonesty and roguery that pass for public service today." I do not recall the rest of our discussion that evening but I left with the firm impression that this charred stone would fit very well in a section of the wall if some Nehemiah should happen along and mobilize a builder to select it.

There is no doubt that a large proportion of Africa's resources are undermined, under-utilized and abused. It seems to me that the most abused and undervalued of the continent's resources is the human one. While the young present potential quarries for the production of the fresh material for the construction of durable walls, there are so many charred stones that lie waste on the rubbish heaps for want of a Nehemiah to shape and integrate in the construction project.

The Horonite does not work alone. From the first, we see him with Tobiah the Ammonite and Geshem the Arab. It is not by chance that we now see all the neighbouring communities arrayed against the Jews and their construction project. The Horonite has been working overtime to mobilize this hostility. Another characteristic of the Horonite is that he is tenacious in his mission. He does not give up on his determination to stop you, discourage you, change your agenda and contain you. And if he finds a chink in your armour or any apparent weakness in your defence, he will use it. We see this as the work progresses and the people begin to feel the strain and stress of continuous labour. Nehemiah records in his memoirs:

Dealing with the Horonite

"Then some of the leaders began complaining that the workmen were tired; and there was so much rubble to be removed that we could never get it done by ourselves. Meanwhile, our enemies were planning to swoop down upon us and kill us, thus ending our work. Whenever the workers who lived in the nearby cities went home for a visit, our enemies tried to talk them out of returning to Jerusalem."

When I started writing this book and aligning my thinking with that of Nehemiah, little did I suspect that in a few short years, we in Nigeria would be literally called upon to rally to the cup-bearer's exhortation to fight for friends, families and homes. I knew that the slippery slope of moral decadence and the total monetization of our thinking in Nigeria and the many other countries of the African region caught up in the throes of corruption did not augur well for our long-term health as nations on the rise.

I had no inkling that the wholesale slaughter of scores of innocent young men and women in their sleep could be carried out with such casual bellicosity in Nigeria. Much more painfully, I could never have imagined that their parents and the leaders of the land whose name I carry as my country would just wring their hands in clueless helplessness.

If someone had mooted it I would have believed, that Nigerians like my brothers in the country that I call my second home, alias Kenya, caught up in the ironic divide between tribe and nation, had the capacity to turn on one another. I had seen this in my child-hood days with the *atemityo* (head-smasher) riots in Tiv Division in 1964 and the *agbekoya* (farmers reject suffering) in the Western region, both of which saw high levels of violence but would never have imagined the ferocity with which we would turn on one another in the 21st century where bloodshed would become a spectator sport.

I know there are those who would balk at my use of the inclusive pronoun in describing the atrocities that have overtaken our land and the iniquity that stalks our waking moments and our dreams. I do that because we are all implicated. We are all victims, actual or potential. We can choose to build when the circumstance and environment afford us the convenience and the wisdom of a Solomon, or build under fire As Nehemiah had to do.

So how does one build under fire, when the enemy appears ubiquitous and unknown? The cup-bearer governor tells his story much better in his own words.

"So I placed armed guards from each family in the cleared spaces behind the walls.

Then as I looked over the situation, I called together the leaders and the people and said to them, 'don't be afraid! Remember the Lord who is great and glorious; fight for your friends, your families and your homes.' Our enemies learnt that we knew of their plot, and that God had exposed and frustrated their plan. Now we all returned to our work on the wall; but from then on, only half worked while the other half stood guard behind them."

When Nehemiah called on the people to trust in God and fight for friend family and home, he was calling on them to remember what could evoke the highest emotional value for them. It was a call that was grounded in that which they held dear and could be called upon to protect with all the power and resources at their command. The exhortation was not sitting on empty words. It was backed up by the practical action of vigilance involving the placement of guards and lookouts who ensured that there was good information and protection for those who were working. In fact, this combination of preparedness for protective action and continued work without interruption became a standard operating procedure for their building under fire.

It is granted that firearm and chemical weapons were not in use in the time of Nehemiah. To confront your enemy in battle array meant you were in plain sight of each other and to kill often meant eyeball to eyeball contact. In our time, a young girl sitting at a computer table thousands of kilometres away can program and manipulate a drone to drop a bomb and wipe out a whole community of people. These are people she has never seen but as blimps on a computer screen that may appear as live one moment and eliminated the next after the bomb has hit its target. In our time, it is possible for one human group to label another as cockroach or vermin and mark them out for destruction. In the time of Nehemiah, a captive, the off-spring of the conquered people could rise to occupy one of the most confidential positions in the court of the most powerful potentate of the time. In our time, purveyors of iniquity imagine zero sum games in which the object of their hatred is wiped out in genocidal pogroms never to exist to cause them annoyance again. In our time, a family can be rudely awakened by gunfire with live bullets sprayed indiscriminately, to cut down the sleeping, the groggily awakening and those running with what they have on their backs, children, women, and men, the young and the old.

So how do you build under fire in our time?

With wisdom and tact, insight, foresight and decisive action, Nehemiah dealt with and overcame the machinations of the Horonite but it was by no means the end. By his very pernicious character and his invidious modus operandi, the Horonite is bound to come at you another way and so he did as we learn when we get back to the memoirs of the cupbearer.

"When Sanballat, Tobiah, Geshem the Arab, and the rest of our enemies found out that we had almost completed the rebuilding of the wall—though we had not yet hung all the doors of the gates—they sent me a message asking me to meet them in one of the villages in the Plain of Ono. But I realized they were plotting to kill me, so I replied by sending back this message to them: 'I am doing a great work! Why should I stop and come and visit with you?'

Four times they sent the same message and each time I gave the same reply. The fifth time, Sanballat's servant came with an open letter in his hand and this is what it said:

"Geshem tells me that everywhere he goes he hears that the Jews are planning to rebel and that is why you are building the wall. He claims you plan to be their king-that is what is being said. He also reports that you have appointed prophets to campaign for you at Jerusalem by saying, "Look! Nehemiah is just the man we need!" you can be very sure that I am going to pass these interesting comments to King Artaxerxes! I suggest that you come and talk it over with me—for that is the only way you can save yourself!"

My reply was, "you know you are lying. There isn't one bit of truth to the whole story. You're just trying to scare us into stopping our work" (O Lord God, please strengthen me!).

Having failed to discourage Nehemiah or stop the work, Sanballat and his allies make desperate attempts to separate Nehemiah from his work, lure him to a meeting in the valley of Ono where they intend no doubt to do him mischief. Nehemiah sees through their plot and refuses to go. Then they pull out their blackmail trump card. A false story is concocted to frighten Nehemiah into a compromise with them. It has become clear that these "poor, feeble Jews" will indeed finish their work in record time. They have been able to effectively counter every subterfuge of Sanballat and his allies but planting a well-calculated rumour in the court of Artaxerxes when Nehemiah is away is another story.

Nehemiah as a court official himself must have known that some people make a very good living from planting pernicious rumours in the courts of rulers. His firm response to this latest threat of Sanballat and his appeal to God indicate that he was not about to fold his arms and watch them tarnish his hard-earned reputation. He was prepared to call their bluff and stand on the truth and his unshakeable confidence in God. I suspect though, that practical man that he was, Nehemiah must have in his tradition of praying and putting a watch, made arrangements to counter any rumour that his enemies would have sought to plant in the court.

In our times, the courts of kings are riddled with spin doctors and image launderers who specialize in manufacturing stories and twisting them to form public opinion. They build up false images of things, individuals or groups and with their allies in the Press, preside over the iniquitous canonization of pernicious falsehood. Called the fourth estate of the realm, supposedly charged with the custodianship of the truth based on an unwavering commitment to the facts the Press often becomes, an oppressive instrument whose agenda is controlled and manipulated by tribal, sectional or oligarchic vested interests?

How does a Nehemiah confront and overcome the pernicious rumours that may be contained in the false open letter carried on the pages of a compromised Press instead of by the hand of the Horonite's servant? As demonstrated by Nehemiah, there is no better antidote against falsehood than the truth backed up by faith in the absolute wisdom and goodness of God and His faithfulness in recognizing and honouring the truth.

One would have thought that Sanballat would now accept defeat. Never! The Horonite is most persistent in his pernicious task. The cupbearer turned governor carries on with the story in his memoirs.

"A few days later I went to visit Shemaiah (son of Delaiah, who was the son of Mehetabel), for he said he was receiving a message from

God. 'Let us hide in the temple and bolt the door,' he exclaimed, 'for they are coming tonight to kill you.' But I replied "should I, the governor, run away from danger?" And if I go into the temple, not being a priest, I would forfeit my life. No, I won't do it.' Then I realized that God had not spoken to him but Tobiah and Sanballat had hired him to scare me and make me sin by fleeing to the temple, and then they would be able to accuse me. 'O my God,' I prayed, 'don't forget the evil of Tobiah, Sanballat, No-adiah the prophetess and all the other prophets who have tried to discourage me.'

It is evident that Sanballat and his allies were well versed in the game of intrigue and influential enough to penetrate even Nehemiah's inner circle to acquire a 'prophet for hire'. This 'prophet' came up with an elaborate scheme to frighten and incriminate Nehemiah by getting him to go hide in the temple to escape imminent death from his enemies. It is worth noting that Nehemiah knew the tradition and the law. He had no right as a non-priest to go into the temple and bolt the door in the name of security. Secondly, he knew that if he the governor started running scared, then how could the people that he had motivated to rise and build ever have confidence in him again? He realized that as governor, he had to overcome the fear of death, in fact be prepared to die for the cause that he believed in. 'Should I, the governor, run away from danger?' he asks the hired prophet.

We shall soon turn our attention to the actual work of building the wall that Nehemiah mobilized his people to do. However, I would first like to point out another aspect of the Horonite's character. We have already seen that he will stop at nothing and use those around you to sabotage your best efforts. If you permit me, we shall fast forward a bit towards the end of the memoirs. The wall has been completed and after establishing a functioning administration in Jerusalem, Nehemiah takes a well-deserved home leave to return to Shushan and touch base with the court before returning for the continuation of his posting in Judah. But look what he found on his arrival. In his own words: ' . . . Eliashib the priest, who had been appointed as custodian of the temple storerooms and who was also a good friend of Tobiah, had converted a storage room into a beautiful guest room for Tobiah'.

Can you imagine it? Tobiah who had taken part in every plot against the work of rebuilding the wall and was the one to come up with the most graphic mocking phrases was occupying a luxurious guest room, not just in the Jerusalem that he had scorned but right inside the temple, courtesy of the high priest. One thing is clear. The Horonite will not give up. Do not expect him to be ashamed after you have defeated him in one battle. Don't expect him to slink off with his tail between his legs and give you a wide berth to satisfy your heart's desire. In fact after you have fought successfully against his every subterfuge and set up something of value, you will find that he and his gang will be the first to jump at the benefits created by your hard labour. He will penetrate and seek to corrupt your system, acquire and use your own trusted or authority figures against you. And sometimes he will succeed.

SEVENTEEN ANTI-HORONITE STRATEGIES

From the memoirs of the cupbearer so far, some lessons have emerged on how to deal with the Horonite determined to ensure you fail. We can identify seventeen of them from Nehemiah's account.

1. Have a clear goal
2. Have a great work in hand
3. Obtain the highest approval
4. Do your reconnaissance in secret
5. Obtain a beast of burden
6. Find a faithful servant
7. Anticipate opposition
8. Report to the highest authority
9. Develop a network around the goal
10. Share the work
11. Banish fear
12. Be ready to die
13. Keep a detailed account
14. Avoid grabiosis
15. Confront evil in public

16. Delegate on merit
17. Pray without ceasing.

Have a clear goal

A clear goal simply states a desired result to be attained through effort in a clear and concise manner that all those who need to work for its attainment can clearly understand it. The scope of a goal can be personal or global and anything in-between. In the case of Nehemiah, it was stated simply in a few words: "You know full well the tragedy of our city; it lies in ruins and its gates are burned. Let us rebuild the wall of Jerusalem and rid ourselves of this disgrace."

Nehemiah's goal was stated simply enough for the political and religious leaders as well as the people who would be doing the work to understand it clearly. Their response was also direct and simple. "They replied at once, 'Good! Let's rebuild the wall' and so the work began." Having a clear goal though can present a challenge in many ways.

A Syndrome Called Angerakuzengezengezong

I grew up in the hills, the plains and the valleys of the Nigerian Benue River in the second half of the Twentieth Century. I have, thanks to the Nigerian Television Authority and the African Radio Television Union, URTNA, travelled widely in my country and Africa at large. I have interacted with the youth and the men and women of my generation for the better part of four decades. And as I write, the men and women of my generation still play a significant part in the affairs of our nation as the movers and shakers of the land. The men and women of my generation and their immediate successors hold the reins of power at virtually every level across the world. In my interactions with them, I have become acutely aware of what I call the ***Angerakuzengezengezong*** syndrome. I have become acutely aware of it because I have had to fight it most of my working life. This is a tendency to seek to impress one's audience with one's knowledge rather than effectively convey meaning in communication. It is important to understand the syndrome because the men and women of my generation who are the decision makers are largely still caught up in its throes. The reality is that while they may be most sincere in their desires to make a positive difference to the circumstances of their people, they might be hampered by their failure to define and articulate clear goals that grab the imagination of those with whom they have to work. Let me explain a little bit about the syndrome.

For those who grew up in the decade of the 50s and 60s in most parts of British colonial Africa, the thirst for grandiloquence in the Queen's language was pervasive. Our heroes of the age in the West African region of her imperial majesty's domain; like Kwame Nkrumah, Nnamdi Azikiwe, Herbert Macaulay and the Enahoros were all masters of the English word and we longed to model our expression after their bombastic styles.

In most parts of the British Empire in Africa, the missionaries played a very important part in formal education. In my part of the world, there was competition between the catholic and protestant missions in their educational programs. Invariably there was stiff competition between the pupils from the Catholic and Protestant schools. Pupils competed on the sports field and then retired to the sidelines or the market places to engage in competitions in the fluent speaking of the English language. At these competitions, popularly known as "*shon*", the meaning was not the issue. The boy—it was invariably boys—who could drop the longest words with the greatest confidence and fluency was the winner of the competition.

Young men scoured the dictionaries for the longest words they could memorize. Some of those who were fortunate to have older siblings in secondary schools that were few and far between had an added advantage. They could scour through their elder siblings' biology textbooks for fabulous zoological and botanical names that they used to bamboozle their hapless mates with. Nobody cared what the long words meant or whether they constituted anything meaningful in intelligent speech.

The audience consisting of peasant farmers and their wives did not know a single word of the Queen's language anyway. The excitement of the *shon* was in the impression.

In the mid-fifties, in the rural primary school of Pika, there was a brazen young man by the name of Iortswam Nev, Di-Nev to his friends. He was an undisputed *shon* champion in his school. Since the words in the Queen's language had a tendency to prove themselves too short when he needed them to clinch a *shon* competition, Di-Nev decided to invent some of his own. It happened one day when Pika, the protestant school had not done too well on the sports field against Adebo, the Catholic school. They would have to do something drastic in the *shon* if they hoped to draw any applause that day. The battle lines were drawn in the dry sandy concourse of Akpagher market. Di-Nev found himself face to face with the pesky Orakem, the square-headed weaverbird of Adebo, so nicknamed because of the way he could send intimidating English words tumbling out of his mouth like a chattering weaverbird. If such words happened to be botanical or zoological words couched in ancient Latin that had been memorized from a Biology textbook, well, that was an "insignificant coincidental".

"Cascara sagrada, carica papaya" Orakem opened in double-barreled fashion.

"You higgledy-piggledy boy" Di-Nev countered.

Orakem waited for the applause to die down then jabbing a finger towards his taller opponent's nose he exclaimed in his staccato voice: "Musca domestica! Periplanata Americana!" Di-Nev did not miss a beat. Twirling on his heel and waving an expansive hand to the attentive audience he pronounced as one with profound wisdom: "Oryctolagus cuniculus! Hibiscus Esculentas". As he turned back to face his opponent, he thought he could detect the killer instinct in the eyes of Orakem. As the latest applause died down, Orakem suddenly started pounding the ground with his right foot while he punched his left palm with his right fist as he rattled out a few more words before dropping what would have been the killer word.

"Ipomoea! Thoracic vertebra! Caudal vertebra! Medulla oblongata! Antidisestablishmentarianism!" The applause was deafening. Di-Nev Almost screamed 'foul!' How dare the pesky sneak! Antidisestablishmentarianism was his own word, from his own Collins National Dictionary, bought for him by his Uncle Benjie who had returned from years of service with the Brits in Burma or some such place. He felt cheated. Since he had got his Collins and discovered that word, it was like he had a copyright to it. Nobody had dared use it before especially in *shon* competition against him. That is why he was highly sought after by his schoolmates when there was a competition and that was the word he always dropped as a clincher. So far, nobody had been able to stand it. And now, the pesky sneak of a weaverbird had taken it right out of his mouth and used it against him. And that was when it happened. As the applause died down, the word just sprung into his throat. It was by pure inspiration. It started like a growl in his throat and built itself into a crescendo that left him standing with his hands stretched out and up palms upwards as he pulled himself to his full height and felt as if he could touch the sky.

"Angerakuzenegezengezong! Tyum tyum matityud! I charge in kwijitiv!" Orakem had no further response. The market broke out

in riotous applause as Di-Nev's schoolmates carried him shoulder-high and broke into joyous songs of victory.

> "We are the wonderful people of Pika School
> We are the wonderful people of Pika School
> If by any chance you don't know us
> Better come and learn to know us"

Not only had Di-Nev wiped away the humiliation of Pika's defeat on the sports field, but also he had created a new vocabulary for the ***shon*** competition. The word ***Angerakuzengezengezong*** with all its attachments had passed into official ***shon*** vocabulary from that day on.

I fear that for many of us, the syndrome is still very much alive. While we may impress one another with the academic analysis of the issues and the problems as we perceive them, we need to identify and define the goals simply and clearly enough for the people to say "Good! Let's rebuild the wall!" or "Good! Let's break down the walls." You may wish to ponder on this need within your own specific context. It manifests itself among scholars who may never address any issue in the society or environment around their campus but impress their peers on the other side of the ocean with esoteric analysis in search of publications in learned journals. It manifests itself in the elite that are educated out of their communities and see their education as an exit visa from the community for which they have become too good and which they can neither relate to nor serve.

SHON COMPETITION

Have a Great Work in Hand

When Tobiah and Sanballat sent word to Nehemiah to meet with them in the valley of Ono, his reply was simple. "I am doing great work here where I am. Why should I abandon it to go visiting with you?" If you are focused on a great and good work, you will have no time for the invitation of the Horonite. We humans as a fact of life are always involved in one form of work or another. Not all of this work is great or good. A great deal of it may be petty and even pernicious.

So how does one define or recognize a great and good work? From our study of Nehemiah's mission and work, we can identify certain qualities that are associated with a great and good work.

It does not focus on self

If Nehemiah had focused his attention on his personality and position as cup-bearer to the most influential potentate of the time in his part of the world; he probably would have made no move that might just jeopardize his position. Since his position required absolute confidentiality and trust with the ruler, he might have questioned the wisdom of giving a clue to the ruler that his sentiments and loyalty might first be to the land of his ancestors. He might have considered the threat posed by other ambitious men in the court who would have no doubt been jostling for that precious position of trust with Artaxerxes. He might have asked the question that is so paramount on the minds of those that you have to deal with in Africa's corridors of power and influence: What is in it for me? Invariably, if the primary question at the back of your mind is "What's in it for me?" when you set out on your work, it can neither be great nor good.

Selfishness demeans and minimizes. It stunts vision to the libidinous or avaricious appetite of one person in the place of the possibilities that are posed by the entirety of human potential. In focusing on the good that can be done for the community, the polity or indeed the entirety of humanity, the vision is expanded and the good that can be attained grows in quantum. A great and good work does not focus on self.

It is not done alone

The conception of a great and good work may be seeded in the recesses of a single mind. Once it has been brought into existence, it must be made to draw and attract the synergy that propels it to the realization of the potential with which it has been born. From Nehemiah's example, we see just how much synergy was drawn in from the diverse, multi-faceted but also multi-talented and multi-endowed groups that were motivated to come out and build beginning with Artaxerxes Longimanus who gave the word to set the process in motion.

It is also not done alone in the sense that we have to recognize the pre-eminence of God in the affairs of the universe. As human beings, we may have the tendency to get carried away by the lure of our own self-importance, our brilliance and apparent omniscience and forget that but for the grace of God, we would have neither the means or occasion to do the great and good work with which we have been entrusted. Nehemiah had the humility to recognize that it was neither his influence, guile, nor persuasive skill that got the emperor to respond positively to his request. You may wish to note from his narration the fact that before responding to the question put by the emperor, he paused to send a quick appeal to the Almighty for guidance before opening his mouth. And when the emperor responded positively, he had the discernment to recognize that it was the spirit of the highest God that was working in the heart of the emperor to give him the support that he needed.

A great and good work requires the mobilization of other human beings whose contribution is vital to its realization but above all the recognition that it is God who has planted its seed in the heart. We have to continue to work with Him. A great and good work is not done alone.

It takes total commitment

Therefore I stationed some of the people behind the lowest points of the wall at the exposed places, posting them by families, with their swords, spears and bows. After I looked things over, I stood up and said to the nobles, the officials and the rest of the people "Don't be afraid of them. Remember the Lord, who is great and awesome, and fight for your brothers, your sons and your daughters, your wives and your homes."

When our enemies heard that we were aware of their plot and that God had frustrated it, we all returned to the wall, each to his own work. From that day on, half of my men did the work, while the other half were equipped with spears, shields, bows and armour. The officers posted themselves behind all the people of Judah who were building the wall.

Those who carried materials did their work with one hand and held a weapon in the other, and each of the builders wore his sword at his side as he worked. But the man who sounded the trumpet stayed with me. Then I said to the nobles, the officials and the rest of the people, "The work is extensive and spread out, and we are widely separated from each other along the wall. Wherever you hear the sound of the trumpet, join us there. Our God will fight for us!"

So we continued the work with half the men holding spears, from the first light of dawn till the stars came out. At that time I also said to the people, "Have every man and his helper stay inside

Jerusalem at night, so they can serve us as guards by night and workmen by day." Neither I nor my brothers nor my men nor the guards with me took off our clothes; each had his weapon, even when he went for water. [b] The cup-bearer's narrative paints a picture of threats from the outside, discouragement from within, rumours of impending attacks and mass slaughter planned by surrounding enemies against the band of weary workers. It is enough to frighten and discourage anyone without total commitment.

There is the commitment of the mind. The steps that Nehemiah takes to counter the plot of the enemy show careful thought and strategic manoeuvre. His use of the existing family structures as his units of organization both for the work and defence eliminated some of the problems that might arise in coming up with new structures and orders. It also provided reinforcement for the commitment of the heart that provided a natural interlocking mobilization strategy.

He reminded them that they were preparing to fight not just for the defence of a half-built wall, but for their "brothers, your sons and your daughters, your wives and your homes." He reminded them that a great and awesome God was on their side. It will be difficult to find a more simple, direct and effective appeal to the heart when it is truly anchored on family, home and God. There is the commitment of the body as the workers arm themselves in readiness for combat when necessary without flagging their effort on the substantive work. A great and good work takes total single-minded commitment.

It is done night and day

Nehemiah and his workers were prepared to work night and day without change of clothes or bath in all the discomfort that one can imagine to hasten the achievement of their objective. A great and good work becomes part of your corporate personality. There is no differentiation or compartmentalization. There is no official personality during the day and private personality during the night. A great and good work disposes of the masks and pretensions and exposes you to scrutiny from within and without.

In the late 1970s I was cutting my teeth in the Nigerian Television system under the tutelage of the indomitable Tom Adaba, the one and only programme controller of the first colour television station in Nigeria and Ibrahim Adamu, the debonair news controller of the station. The two heads of content creation and their astute Egyptian General Manager, Dr. Girgis Salama allowed us, the young bunch of creative and sometimes fiery heads in the system a lot of latitude to experiment and generate interesting and challenging content. With the likes of Abdulkarim Mohamed Abdullahi, Joe Edebiri, Ben Orewere, Dennis Akpede and Yakubu Mohamed, we went to town.

One of the programs that came out of my brainstorming with Abdulkarim was a do-it-yourself show called "Give it a Try" which I produced and presented. It featured a wide range of things that you could do at home to save money, expand your skills base or just chase away boredom. Well, one evening, I did not take my own good advice and went out with a couple of friends to Havana Hotel, a popular watering joint in the heart of the tin city of Jos. Behind Havana was a rather extensive red light district where anything and quite a lot could and did happen. Emboldened by a couple or maybe a triplet of cold beers, we stepped out into the murky atmosphere of the rear side of Havana Hotel. As we picked our way through the skimpily-clad and sloe-eyed young women and sly young and not so young men out for the catch of the night or maybe a short time acquaintance, the crying of a young woman a little bit to our left caught my attention. I moved towards the direction and soon saw a young man of about my age beating one of the skimpily-clad girls very brutally. My sense of justice and chivalry offended, revulsion at violence against women and all, I took a few quick steps and laid a restraining hand on the man's shoulder. He turned angrily with a raised fist, took one look at me and spat out: "Mr. Give it a try. None of your business!" He pulled his girlfriend or whoever away and left me the "Teevee star" the new centre of attention as the crawlers of the red light district converged to take a closer look at this Mr. Give it a Try who was interfering in what was none of his business. I had to very self-consciously find a quick exit from the scene.

I was not involved in what could be described as a great and good work. However, my exposure as a Television producer/presenter on the first colour television station in Nigeria made me a bit of a public figure. The brutal young man clearly did not expect to see me in the red light district of Jos. "We associate you with the clean romantic and glamorous image of the first colour television station. What the hell are you doing in this place at this hour?"

Make no mistake. If you are to be involved in the planning and implementation of a great and good work, you have to be prepared to work at it night and day under scrutiny.

It will be opposed

There will always be no shortage of Sanballats, Tobiahs and Geshems to oppose every great and good work that you embark upon. That is the nature of things in this plane. The preponderance of negativity on earth ensures that every anomalous situation has its benefactors who will get up in arms against you when you try to change the status quo. More often than not, they will conceal their arms but stand eagle-eyed for an opportunity to stab you in the back when your attention is distracted even a little. Your great and good work will be opposed directly or indirectly. Some of the kind of opposition that you will face is demonstrated in the work of modern Sanballats in the stories that follow.

Sanballats at Work Today

Permit me to divert a little to give you a modern Sanballat story. It happened in an African community in an African country that shall for the moment remain nameless.

A Lucrative Business

The Nehemiah in this story is alive and well and still working for the United Nations. However the Sanballats and Tobiahs with whom he had to contend were so effective in their opposition that at the end of the day, he returned to his nuclear family in the Western capital where he is based and has effectively given up on trying to "save" his community.

Africans who work for the United Nations System are some of the best and brightest of the continent. They come from the universities, the research institutes and some of the more successful non-governmental organizations usually with a track record of some original work and thought. There are also those who come from the diplomatic service. Some of these usually enter the higher echelons of the international civil service, having rubbed shoulders with the decision-makers and lobbied over time to be appointed to those exalted positions.

You will find invariably that at all levels of the organization, the international system extracts its pound of flesh, blood and bone with water to boot. In some of the agencies, even getting to spend time with one's nuclear family is like a privilege that should be indulged sparingly. You will also find that the dizzying height to which an African has risen in the service is not necessarily an indication of the power or influence that he or she can exercise. Although an international civil servant is not supposed to take orders or directives from any other source but the hierarchy of his or her service, in reality, he who pays the piper dictates the tune.

In a situation where some African countries get the travelling and participation costs of their delegations to sensitive trade negotiations and other crucial meetings paid by other countries, it can hardly be expected that they would deviate radically from the tunes of their sponsors. International civil servants from such countries that may also fail to pay their annual dues to these organizations for years hardly have a voice in the system. They can apply their skill and intelligence to doing the technical work especially when it is DDD (Difficult, Degrading and Dangerous).

After years of having their asses kicked and their heads straightened by the international system, they become quite alienated from their African origins. Back home, they may be seen as African Europeans which is another way of saying you are a naïve nuisance or worse. Since their wanderings through the trouble spots of the world allow them little time to connect with the home front, they may become quite disconnected from the realities of their origins. While some heighten this disconnection by preferring to spend their holidays in the pleasure spots of the world, there are those who retain the African habit of not going on holidays but merely taking leave.

After they contribute their pound of flesh and blood cooped up in offices that enjoy artificial light or cubicles that belong to whatever agency has allocated them some square footage and one or two windows for twelve calendar months, they go on leave. They hike off to some village in the rain forest; the savannah or scrublands where they keep themselves extremely busy solving the problems of the extended family and the clan. They may also pass the time fending off the forays of those of their not so nice kinsmen who might want to lay hands on and snatch the fabulous wealth that they may be perceived to have acquired. It can be a mixed bag of pressure and stress that bears no approximation to some leisurely gambolling on a Greek beach.

During those twenty-something days, they may go "home" and immerse themselves in community life, forcing their kith and kin to a month of drama and acting until the African Europeans go back to their perches in the land of the Bature.

Our Nehemiah was such an African European. He has been in the international system for more than 20 years without completely losing touch with home. On leave in his home village that is yet to boast of running water and connection to the national electricity grid, he noticed that children and infants in his and the surrounding villages were dropping dead from diarrhoea. He swung into action.

After a rapid assessment of the situation confirmed that the children were indeed dying from dehydration caused by diarrhoea, he contacted his UNICEF peers in the local state office for help. They were only too willing to be of assistance to a colleague of the International Civil Service. An allocation paper was given to him to pick up a sizeable quantity of oral re-hydration packages from the medical stores of the agency to take care of the diarrhoea problem in his community. His further contribution was to make the arrangements for the transportation of the consignment to his community.

He decided to pick up the medical officer from the medical centre in his village and hand over the allocation paper to him for collection. That problem solved, or so he thought, he now went about the other crowded programs of his leave. So our friend went off attending to the other important commitments of his crowded agenda, confident that the nasty problem of diarrhoea in his community had been taken care of.

A couple of weeks into his leave, he threw a party to which virtually everyone who was anyone in the village was invited. One of the doctors who also worked in the medical centre approached him several times during the evening to request for confidential audience. Our friend eventually told him if he waited until the other guests had left, they could talk. Since the guests were in no hurry to leave, it was not until the wee hours that international civil servant and medical officer sat down to talk.

"Hey Prof. Chucks" the doctor started with a familiar air forcing our friend to take a second look at this man who addressed him with the familiarity of his primary school days. Everybody in his class and some of the senior boys called him Prof because of the thick glasses that he had started wearing at a very young age due to his very poor sight. He felt slightly irritated at this man recalling his primary school memories and all the insecurities that that era of his life evoked with that name. Thirty-odd years later and oozing confidence from every pore of his body and buoyed on by the laser surgery that had corrected his congenital eye defect and the several UN promotions that had already put him in a D1 position under the age of 50, as he looked in the doctor's eyes, recognition at last sprang to his consciousness.

"Uzo! You old rascal!" It had indeed been many years. Uzodinma had been a bully in primary school but for some reason, he had had a soft spot for Chukwuma otherwise known as Prof Chuks. His mind went back to those days when Uzo had got him out of the oppressive clutches of other bullies only to convert him into his courier to the girls. Lost in thought for a while, he was brought back to the present by the accusing tone in Uzodinma's voice.

"How could you" Uzo was emphasizing with passion in his voice, "bring such a fantastic business to this village and bypass your old buddy to give it to a stranger? How could you Chucks?"

Chucks protested that he had no idea what his childhood friend was talking about. It took Uzo quite a while to believe that Chuks was earnest in his denials.

"You mean you are not aware that Dr. Kelechi has already changed his old banger of a Peugeot for a brand new Tokunbo Toyota Camry and even bought a nice Honda Halla for his wife? You mean you don't know that Dr. Kelechi has almost completed the house that he has been struggling with for the past three years all because of the business you introduced him to only two weeks ago? I beg Chuks; I am not asking you to give me the same deal. Even half will satisfy me. In fact, whatever I get, I am prepared to share with you fifty-fifty. In fact you can have sixty and I will be satisfied with forty."

It turned out that immediately after the innocent international civil servant had turned the allocation paper over to the health centre medical doctor, the man had done a quick mental calculation and concluded that his money had come. Half a million sachets of oral re-hydration salts at twenty Naira per sachet meant a cool ten million naira in his pocket. Ten Million Naira could make a lot of things happen in the village and beyond. Before he had even got back to the clinic to take the supply truck that he decided to drive himself to collect the consignment, he had stopped at the chemists and drugstores in the town and in the towns on the way and collected confirmed orders (COD) for the entire consignment. He delivered the oral re-hydration salts, collected his money and drove the virtually empty delivery van back to the health centre and went home with a *"Ghana must go!"* full of money to celebrate with his wife.

As the story based on the circumstantial evidence provided by Uzo fell into place in his mind, an oddity in Dr. Kelechi's behaviour on the day he had handed him the allocation paper popped back into Chukwuma's consciousness with startling clarity. Kelechi had genuflected and thanked him profusely. Naively he had thought the doctor was grateful that he had played a part in putting in his hands the means of stopping the unnecessary deaths of children under his watch from diarrhoea. He had no idea whatsoever, that the man's antics were emanating from the imagination of dancing Naira before his eyes. He was thanking him for putting some ten million cool Naira in his pocket.

Our indignant international civil servant pulled hell and high water to get the council of elders and the board of the health centre to meet the following day. He managed to control his anger long enough to paint a graphic picture of a callous member of the community in a position of trust who betrayed his trust and traded in the blood of dying infants for some Naira to meet his fancies.

Dr. Kelechi did not bother the community with the benefit of a personal appearance. He sent one of the lackeys that his new-found wealth had enabled him to acquire to go and speak on his behalf. "Dr. Kelechi has asked me to convey his unreserved apologies to this august assembly for his inability to attend this meeting due to pressing engagements in the state capital. He asked me to inform the elders that all the cows slaughtered during the recent Christmas party at which they all participated were sourced from the proceeds of the business that he had done with their brother who was sojourning in the land of the white man. He equally asked me to inform the members of the board that the Christmas hampers that they received with the fat brown envelopes of Naira were also sourced from the proceeds of the same business. As for my brother Chukwuma, Dr. Kelechi suspects that he may be headed back to the land of the White Man by the time he returns from his engagements so he thanks him once again for this good business and wishes him a very safe journey back. He hopes that you will have fruitful deliberations."

Our friend who had this Sanballat and Tobiah experience in his home community has found it extremely difficult to identify himself with the possibility of any redeeming feature in the community. "Can you imagine?" he asked me pointedly, "that the throats of the elders and members of the board were so blocked by chunks of beef and their mouths so full of hampers wine that none of them could utter a single word in admonition of Kelechi or in defence of me?"

Onomatopoeic Potholes

Once upon a time in an African country formerly known for its community self-help spirit called Harambee in the Kiswahili language, the roads in a certain part of the capital city fell into serious disrepair. The city had become so famous for its nasty roads in which gigantic potholes hobnobbed with mounds of rubbish that the humour columnists and cartoonists resorted to naming the monstrosities after their city mayors in onomatopoeic rhyme. The mayor under whose watch the potholes came into their own was called Gumo. Since he seemed absolutely powerless to do anything against them, the peripatetic humour columnist who went by the well-loved name of "Whispers son of the soil" christened them Gumo holes and the whole of the city knew them by their first name.

The gentleman who succeeded him was called Kongo. Since the potholes had grown so large and domineering in some parts of the town that when it rained, cars literally had to swim, Whispers rechristened them "Kongo craters".

There was in the capital city one road construction company that owned many heavy trucks that were responsible for the devastation of the roads in one part of the town. In the spirit of Harambee, the management of this company decided that since their trucks were mainly responsible for the state of those roads, and since they were in the business of building roads, they could construct those roads for the community.

"Wait a moment", someone informed them. "You need to obtain the development permission from the appropriate local government authority. You need to get the blessing of city hall otherwise it would be an illegal development that might attract sanctions. Get the permission please."

The management of the company went to city hall to obtain the permission. They thought they would be welcomed with open arms and commended for caring enough to be their brothers' keeper in the matter of the Kongo craters. They were rather taken aback when the appropriate city hall official rubbed his hands avariciously and asked them to bring the money that they had decided to put into the project so that city hall could commission the work according to their specifications.

"You don't understand," the MD of the construction company told the city hall official, "We are civil engineering specialists. We construct roads, bridges and other civil works. We have the equipment and the manpower to do the job ourselves to your specifications. All we need is the specifications that you require for the road and the development permission for same. We will obtain the materials; we will use our machines and personnel to build the road. All we need is your development permission and the specifications that you want."

"O yes we understand. You bring the money and we will contract the job to a competent contractor to do it. After you give us the money, you can tender and if you win, we give you the development permission." He rubbed his hands in that ominous manner again. The MD took his team and went out rubbing his head not quite sure what sort of logic he had just been exposed to. Needless to say, the road was not done.

Five on the Board Equals Ten Million

In another town in another region of the continent, a multinational company involved in the production of soft drinks, approached the government of a region in whose capital they were located. "Our industry as you know uses lots and lots of water. We see that your urban waterworks here are rather small and inadequate for even your current population. Our demand will draw heavily on your resources and render the picture even more serious. We would therefore like to propose a win-win situation where we expand your urban waterworks to the capacity where it can cater to our needs and yours for the next ten years at least without problems. We can claim part of our investment through rebated water bills over time. How would you consider that for private-public partnership?"

"There are five of us on the water board. We will need Two Million each to push this through. Ten Million to us is all it will take." No kudos for guessing whether that waterworks project has taken off or ever will. The last I heard, the personnel of the multinational who were a little stumped as to how they could introduce a hefty figure of ten million into a project that had already been carefully worked out is considering setting up its independent water works while the inhabitants of that industrializing city have to continue struggling with criminally inadequate supplies of the stuff that the Somalis equate with life.

Make no mistake. Your great and good work will be opposed and may even be turned against you. You have to find the means of overcoming the opposition and rising above the negativity. Nehemiah gives some examples worth examining as some of the iniquities of his time were just as dastardly. Listen to the cup-bearer.

> [1]Many of the poor people began to complain against their fellow Jews. [2]Some of them were saying, "We have many children. We must get some grain if we are going to eat and stay alive."
>
> [3]Other people were saying, "This is a time of famine. We have to use our fields, vineyards, and homes to pay for grain."
>
> [4]And still other people were saying, "We have to pay the king's tax on our fields and vineyards. But we

cannot afford to pay, so we are borrowing money to pay the tax. [5]We are as good as the others. Our sons are as good as their sons. But we will have to sell our sons and daughters as slaves. Some of us have already had to sell our daughters as slaves. There is nothing we can do. We have already lost our fields and vineyards. Other people own them now."

[6]When I heard their complaints, I was very angry. [7]I calmed myself down, and then I went to the rich families and the officials. I told them, "You are forcing your own people to pay interest on the money you loan them. You must stop doing that!" Then I called for all the people to meet together [8]and said to them, "Our fellow Jews were sold as slaves to people in other countries. We did our best to buy them back and make them free. And now, you are selling them like slaves again!"

The rich people and officials kept quiet. They could not find anything to say. [9]So I continued speaking. I said, "What you people are doing is not right! You know that you should fear and respect our God. You should not do the shameful things other people do! [10]My men, my brothers, and I are also lending money and grain to the people. But let's stop forcing them to pay interest on these loans. [11]You must give their fields, vineyards, olive fields, and houses back to them, right now! And you must give back the interest you charged them. You charged them one percent for the money, grain, new wine, and oil that you loaned them."

[12]Then the rich people and the officials said, "We will give it back and not demand anything more from them. Nehemiah, we will do as you say."

Then I called the priests. I made the rich people and the officials promise to God that they would do what they said.[13]Then I shook out the folds of my clothes. I said, "God will do the same thing to everyone who does not keep their promise. God will shake them out of their houses and they will lose everything they worked for. They will lose everything!"

I finished saying these things and all the people agreed. They all said, "Amen" and praised the LORD. So the people did as they had promised.

Obtain the Highest Approval

In Nehemiah's time, approval did not come any higher than the Emperor Artaxerxes, also known as the king of kings. Nehemiah had obtained his approval for his great and good work. However, he knew that there was an authority higher than Artaxerxes and so he sought the approval of this higher authority with every step he took. He prayed to God continually on the work in general and on specific issues of decision and action. It is noteworthy however that although Nehemiah had the highest authority in the land as well as the approval of the absolute highest authority in heaven and on earth, he did not flaunt it in the face of his opposition. He retained his humility before God and man in the prosecution of his assignment. Like Nehemiah you will need humility and reliance on the highest of authorities to succeed in your great and good work.

The tendency of my Nigerian siblings is generally to flaunt the "Do you know who I am?" syndrome. Sometimes this can play out with comic absurdity. On the well laid out and pristine boulevards of Abuja, Nigeria's new federal capital, I was riding front seat passenger with an old friend, a gentleman of gentlemen who is now resting in the great beyond. In the back seat was another friend, a senior air force officer. We were approaching an intersection where a traffic policeman was in control. As we slowed down to receive the hand signal from the traffic policemen, a car from the outer lane suddenly swerved in front of us and brushed our front fender before screeching to a halt across two lanes. The young driver, a lady in her mid-twenties flung open the door and came out angrily. First she inspected the damage to her car and then belligerently confronted my friend at the wheel. See the damage to my car? See the damage to my car?

My friend, a volunteer traffic cop in his spare time answered mildly with his trademark smile "You caused it didn't you?" the young lady would not be consoled. "Do you know who you are talking to?" she demanded with the petulance of misplaced authority?

"No Madame, I don't know you but it is obvious you know nothing about traffic rules or the Highway Code. Can I see your driving licence?" My friend makes to open his door and step out of the car. She turns on her heel and calls to somebody in her car. "Jack!" she calls out. "He is asking for my driving licence." The front passenger door of the other car opens and a young man in a Nigerian Air Force lieutenant's uniform steps out of the car no doubt to intimidate these old men who are causing a bother to his darling or whatever. At this point, our back seat passenger also comes out of the car. The young officer recognizes him and immediately salutes but that is not enough for him. He goes flat on his belly on the tarmac dust and all, while apologizing profusely in the way only a Nigerian knows how. Even with the highest authority in the land, don't march forth in arrogance.

Do Your Reconnaissance in Secret

When Nehemiah arrived in Jerusalem, he took the time to study and understand the magnitude of the problem with which he had to contend before embarking on his action. He did his reconnaissance in the dead of night with only a few loyal servants

57

and a dumb donkey on whose back he rode. He did not delegate the assessment of the situation to a third party. He did it himself. In the dead of night locked in his own thoughts, he did not have any discouraging voices with which to contend. With no audience to watch what this high official from the emperor's court was up to, there was no call for any self-consciousness in getting down on all fours to scramble though a narrow crevice or claw his way up a heap of rubble to see what lay on the other side.

Doing his reconnaissance in secret also no doubt gave him a bit of a head start over his enemies who would otherwise have been onto him right from the beginning and probably foiled any attempt at mobilization of the people for the work.

Doing his reconnaissance in secret must also have put Nehemiah in a superior position as far as intimate knowledge of the specific challenges of building the wall were concerned. I don't know but I am definitely sure that most inhabitants of the conquered city did not make it a habit of going round the wall to see how devastated it was. From his secret reconnaissance, I am sure that he had enough first-hand knowledge to impress all the assembled people with convincing descriptions of what he had seen and what could be done to redeem the wall at the various places. It is not likely that the man came out of the woodwork and just told the people "Shame on you! Let's build the wall!" and they responded "Yes let us build." To get a good understanding of the problem and have a chance to develop a strategy for action that has a chance of success, you need to keep your counsel and exercise some strict confidentiality at the initial stages of your great and good work.

Obtain a Beast Of Burden

Nehemiah's beast of burden was a donkey on whose back he rode to move around the devastated walls of Jerusalem. The beast of burden complemented his ability to do the work that he needed to do. In the modern world, the beast of burden may not be a donkey but a skill that you may need to acquire to be able to understand the demands and requirements of your great and good work.

Your preparation may require attending adult education classes in the evenings to acquire knowledge in a specific skill that may be essential in mobilizing your community towards a specific socio-economic goal. It may require learning a new language that enables you to break a communication barrier in your effort to reconcile warring communities.

Your beast of burden will carry you some of the way but there will be some places in your wall where you have to get off your beast of burden and get down on all fours to scramble through difficult terrain and narrow crevices. Your skill or professionalism will not suffice in certain situations. So by all means obtain a beast of burden but be aware of the fact that it will not carry you all the way. If you want to get your great and good work done, you must be prepared to get off your high horse from time to time and scramble through rubble and broken stones on all fours in humility without the self-consciousness of your technical or professional superiority.

Find a Faithful Servant

Nehemiah had some faithful servants who were prepared to go on the reconnaissance night trip with him, who no doubt shared in the challenges of reconnaissance and to support their master in his task. Although you must exercise confidentiality in the initial steps of your great and good work, you must find at least one faithful servant with whom you can share your total vision. Your faithful servant will no doubt have insights that you can draw upon to sharpen your vision. He or she will also be there to help articulate your vision should, God forbid, anything happen to you. Find a faithful servant.

Finding and retaining a faithful servant is not an easy task. Of the prophets whose exploits are reported in the books of the prophets in the Bible, there is high praise for the exploits of Elijah the Tishbite. He performed seven spectacular miracles including calling down fire from heaven and raising a young man from the dead. However, Elisha who had been his faithful servant doubled the score with 14 miracles because he had asked for and been given a double portion of Elijah's spirit.

There was a young man who stood in line to continue this great prophetic tradition if he had only been patient enough to bide his time and ask for a double portion of Elisha's spirit. His name was Gehazi. This potential giant of the spirit however ended up as a leper with a curse to carry the dreaded disease and pass it down his lineage from generation to generation because of the lust for temporary gratification. The story of how Gehazi moved from "most promising candidate" to "the accursed one" is told in the book of Chronicles. The story of this servant who did not live up to his expected faithfulness to his master and indeed to the ultimate master is only mentioned here to illustrate how difficult it can be to recruit and train a faithful servant.

In the unfolding digital age that we have been privileged to witness in our time, this difficulty has been surmounted by the possibilities created by the new media of communication and social networks. It is possible through these new channels to quickly build up a following of like-minded people who are prepared to work with you for a cause or an idea to which they subscribe. The faithfulness in this case will not be to you as a person but to the idea that you represent or speak for. The many faithful servants united around an idea will carry forward the great and good work that you have started. There will certainly be some Gehazis among the following that you generate but they can never be in the majority.

Anticipate Opposition

Nehemiah's strategy for approaching the work indicated that he anticipated some opposition and was prepared to deal with it practically in a timely manner. When you embark on a great and good work, you must be aware that there are those who have a definite vested interest in whatever anomalous situation you may be trying to straighten out and they will fight you. The story of the onomatopoeic potholes aptly illustrates this truth.

Report to the Highest Authority

Judah was not exactly one of the central provinces of the empire. Having taken up the job of rebuilding the walls of his beloved Jerusalem, Nehemiah was no doubt cut off for a while from the palace of Artaxerxes. He knew however that he had an authority higher than the emperor to whom he could report and he did this at every important turn. Whether he was sending a prayer arrow heavenwards before responding to a query or putting a matter before God for adjudication, Nehemiah made sure that he was reporting his progress, challenges and steps to victory to God at all times.

It is good to keep the highest human authority aware of your great and good work and its progress but it is even more important to report to the highest authority that supersedes all other authorities, God himself. Report to the highest authority; be specific in your requests, supplication and intercession.

Develop a Network around the Goal

The list of those who were mobilized for the work is impressive. It encompasses neighbourhood groups, professional associations, religious orders and associations, artisans, peasants, families. There were groups that were joined together in the work through mutual interests and proximity. They constituted natural networks for the execution of specific segments of the work. It is also noteworthy that as the work progressed; other issues arose that had to be dealt with thus strengthening the social structure of the community. As long as Nehemiah was able to focus the minds and energies of the people on the goal that was larger than their individual ones, the work progressed in spite of all the challenges. Develop a network around the goal.

Share the Work

In the third chapter of Nehemiah's memoirs, we have a detailed account of all those who took part in the construction of the various segments of the wall. There is no detailed account of the meetings that must have taken place with the various construction teams to coordinate their work both technically and administratively. The fact that the work was progressing smoothly and great progress was being made in record time is proof that the technical and administrative coordination was effectively done. The sharing of the work also showed that everyone was involved where he or she could work effectively and conveniently. If you have to repair the wall in front of your house or join hands with your neighbour to construct a section of the wall that debuts on your common border, it is much more convenient than being taken to a place that might be foreign to you. Share the work with convenience and effectiveness in mind. But sometimes this is easier said than done. In management, sharing the work is sometimes called delegation.

Delegation involves trusting a colleague or subordinate to have enough knowledge and responsibility to replace you on the job. It involves sharing the knowledge and skills that you have so that your subordinates can become as effective as you are. Although its advantages are so obvious, for some it does not come easy as illustrated in the case of the three Nigerian managers.

Three Nigerian Managers

In Nigeria, the story is told of an interview that took place in Lagos in the days when that megalopolis was the capital of the country. Three regional managers were invited to the capital to interview for promotion to higher positions. The interview board had only one question for each of the three candidates. "Mr. Yakubu," they started with the first candidate, "Now that you are here, what is happening to your job back in Kaduna?"

"No problem sirs. My deputy is a very competent gentleman. I have trained him well and he can fill in for me on the routine matters effectively. In fact, the only matters that might have to wait for me are those that may be above his discretionary signature level. I am confident that if I were to be moved from the station, he can replace me without a problem."

"Mr. Lasisi," they asked the second candidate, "now that you are here for this interview, what is happening to your job back there in Lokoja?"

"The work is going on smoothly sirs. I have an open line of communication with my deputy and his deputy. Wherever I am, they can be in touch with me on the phone and by fax on any important matters. Routine matters they can handle without problems."

"Mr. Okeke, for this time that you are attending this interview here in Lagos, what is happening to your job back in Enugu?" they asked the third candidate.

"My brothers," he said with a lament in his voice, "for these three days that I am here, I can only imagine the mess those boys must be creating. When I get back, I am definitely sure it will take me at least a whole week to undo the damage they will have perpetrated in this time."

No kudos for guessing who got their promotions and who was sent back to his all-important job of undoing the mess of others. When you share the work effectively, you will have no messes to clean up because you will have built the capacities and given the training that is needed to have your team on course and contributing their input without friction or inefficiency. Share the work effectively.

Banish Fear

Nehemiah not only showed his willingness to fight for what he believed was a great and good work but also took steps to banish fear from his work force starting with himself. The cup-bearer and governor in his own succinct way tells us how he dealt with the plot to instil fear into him and dramatically end his mission with possible disgrace to boot.

"One day I went to the house of Shemaiah son of Delaiah, the son of Mehetabel, who was shut in at his home. He said, "Let us meet in the house of God, inside the temple, and let us close the temple doors, because men are coming to kill you—by night they are coming to kill you."

But I said, "Should a man like me run away? Or should one like me go into the temple to save his life? I will not go!"

Be Ready to Die

Leaders who have overcome the fear of death become truly invincible in the successful pursuit of their great and good works. I am not here referring to the twisted form of deluded self-glorification that is associated with the manipulated hate-filled psyches of suicide bombers. Leaders who genuinely seek the good of others and immerse themselves in great and good works inspired by the spirit of love beyond the fear of death are prepared to face death in the pursuit of their missions. They are the ones who leave legacies that endure. Mahatma (great soul) Ghandi is one example from modern history whose overcoming of the fear of death led him to leaving a lasting legacy to his subcontinent of India and an example of non-violent resistance to injustice that has inspired others across the world.

Our contemporary history has turned up another figure whose larger than life stature and the legacy that it has created are bound to move from historical fact to heroic legend for generations to come across the whole world. In a brief response to the charge of high treason that he faced in a British South African court that had the unchallengeable power to sentence him to death, Nelson Mandela demonstrated what it means to overcome the fear of death because your great and good work has consumed your fear.

He said,

> "During my lifetime I have dedicated myself to this struggle of the African people. I have fought against white domination, and I have fought against black domination. I have cherished the ideal of a democratic and free society in which all persons live together in harmony with equal opportunities. He paused and looked at the judge and added,

It is an ideal which I hope to live for and achieve.

Then, dropping his voice, he concluded:

But, if needs be, it is an ideal for which I am prepared to die." (Sampson 1999, 192)

By daring to step beyond the border prescribed by the fear of death, Nelson Mandela did not die but lived and went on in the struggle to see his country freed from the clutches of apartheid and him installed as leader of the New South Africa. By being prepared to die for what he believed in, he not only escaped death but lived to see the practical realization of those ideals for which he was prepared to live and to die.

The Master Jesus, the embodiment of love who lived for only 33 years in the remote province of the Roman empire known as Judea and whose work spanned the short space of three years of itinerant preaching without a place to lay his head, who actually went all the way and died a horrible death on the cross has left a legacy that prophet or avatar is yet to equal.

In your commitment to the accomplishment of your great and good work, you must allow your strong commitment to it to consume your fear of death.

Keep a detailed account

Accountability and integrity go together. In chapter 7 of the memoirs of Nehemiah, there is a detailed account of the inhabitants and their genealogies and a detailed account of what the heads of families contributed to the work in money and materials down to the last drachma of gold and mina of silver, not to mention the camels, mules and donkeys.

The record shows that while the cup-bearer turned governor had the right to exact taxes and apply them to both the work and his own expenses, he chose rather to give than to receive. By keeping a detailed account of what he did, he forestalled any temptation that one might have of accusing him. Of course we see that in spite of his transparency and integrity, the Horonite was able to concoct a story of rebellion that might sound believable in Shushan. Although you cannot stop the Horonite from concocting his stories, your transparent accounting will stand you in good stead when it matters most. Keep a detailed account of your transactions.

Avoid Grabiosis

In some countries in Africa, there is a division of the major ethnic groups into the people of Bantu and Nilotic stock. It appears as if the Nilotic generally produce the pastoral communities while the Bantus are generally agriculturalists. For some other reasons whose genesis may be lost in antiquity, the pastoralists tend to look down on the tenders of the land and growers of crops. It may have something to do with the story of Cain the tiller of the land, and Abel the keeper of the flock and all that. In some African communities, this antagonism between the pastoralists and the agriculturalists leads to perennial bouts of violent conflict and bloodletting that pose serious challenges to government. In one country where the pastoralists were in power for a very long period and lorded it over the agriculturalists, the frustrated underdogs coined the expression "pastoral economics". The term was used to describe the antics of their inept government's general mismanagement of the public sector, especially the government parastatals. The top management positions in these government companies were doled out to political and tribal cronies without consideration for their competence or productivity.

Pastoral Economics and Grabiosis

In pastoral economics, the herder looks out for the places where the grass is green and leads his flock to eat their fill as long as it remains green. As soon as they have turned it brown with their merciless eating, they move on and look out for the next green field. The story was that any government company that was doing very well was likely to have its top management replaced with people that were mainly from the head of state's ethnic group. They would invariably run it to the ground. As soon as it became distressed or insoluble, the key management people would be promoted to another green grass corporation while someone from the agricultural or fishing communities would be brought in to return it to green for another round of eating.

Another term coined by the cartoonists and humour columnists to describe the insatiable appetites of their political leaders for the looting of public funds and property is *"grabiosis"*. Grabiosis is characterized by a roving eye that cannot endure the sight of any prime land without the desire to grab it quickly and put a building on it whether it had already been earmarked as a park, public toilet facility or burial ground. It could also belong to some legitimate owner who was not powerful enough to resist the grabiosis sufferer's firm grab and snatch movement. There is no limit to the hunger and thirst of the grabiosis sufferer to the amount of property that he or she can acquire to be satisfied. A combination of pastoral economics and grabiosis of course ensures that countries and communities whose leaders are subjected to both remain in perpetual under-development.

Nehemiah had every temptation to become infected with grabiosis. He had the imperial sanction to grab whatever he could if he so desired and legitimately also. The cup-bearer turned governor gives us his own account of how he avoided grabiosis and the steps he took to stop the privileged in the community from entrenching it as their code of transaction with the less fortunate of their brothers and sisters.

"Moreover, from the twentieth year of King Artaxerxes, when I was appointed to be their governor in the land of Judah, until his thirty-second year—twelve years—neither I nor my brothers ate the food allotted to the governor.

But the earlier governors—those preceding me—placed a heavy burden on the people and took forty shekels of silver from them in addition to food and wine. Their assistants also acted as lords over the people. But out of reverence for God I did not act like that. Instead, I devoted myself to the work on this wall. All my men were assembled there for the work; we did not acquire any land.

Furthermore, a hundred and fifty Jews and officials ate at my table, as well as those who came to us from the surrounding nations. Each day one ox, six choice sheep and some poultry were prepared for me, and every ten days an abundant supply of wine of all kinds. In spite of all this, I never demanded the food allotted to the governor, because the demands were heavy on these people."

Seldom will one find a leader who is prepared to be as self-sacrificing as Nehemiah to the point of forfeiting even his legitimate entitlement in consideration of the people's plight. On the contrary, the president of an impoverished African country justifies his acquisition of a presidential jet while the majority of his constituents are living below the poverty line on the grounds that he deserves that convenience as head of state. That Nehemiah was able to avoid grabiosis and leave that example shows it can be done in appropriate circumstances. And there are examples in our recent history.

Mwalimu and the Ghanaian

Mwalimu Julius Nyerere who straddled the affairs of his native Tanzania for more than three decades left no mansion behind. As president, he took a mortgage loan like any of his ordinary *talakawa* and paid his instalments as and when due to completion on the simple dwelling that was his home until his dying day. No kudos for guessing who among his contemporaries who were steeped in looting the resources of the land for themselves and their pernicious offspring has left a more enduring positive legacy. Grabiosis can and should be avoided.

A few years ago, I met a remarkable Ghanaian who gave me an insight into some of the dynamics that had led to a transformation of that country into a much gentler version of its brash big brother in the West African region. In the traumatic years of the 70s when a cocky young air force officer grabbed power for the second time in less than a decade, lined up three past heads of state with several other senior military officers and shot them, a combination of fear and boiling anger swept across the land. A large number of Ghanaians left the country to find refuge in the West African region and beyond. The people's tribunals that were set up to try and summarily deal with offenders against the polity sent many people to the great beyond for all sorts of real or imagined offences that might range from chicken theft to possession of the evil eye or a big car. The fear of Jerry Rawlings and the summary justice of the people's tribunals led some people to put as much mileage as possible between themselves and any government job of whatever description.

It was at this time that our friend was invited and asked by no less a person than the Commander in Chief himself to take up the job of permanent secretary in a rather sensitive ministry of the government. He eventually agreed to take the appointment subject to certain conditions. He would draw no salary. He did not want to be saddled with any financial responsibility that would require appending his signature to a cheque or other financial document. He would require three months of annual leave to go and earn money from his consultancies to sustain his essential lifestyle while donating his time to work for the government of Ghana. He told me that several highly qualified Ghanaians similarly donated their time and skill without pay to bring their country out of the woods.

MWALIMU JULIUS NYERERE

NELSON MANDELA

GEN. AKUFFO

GEN. ACHEAMPONG

JERRY RAWLINGS

GEN. AFRIFA

Jerry Rawlings of Ghana and the Military Heads of State executed
by his regime.

Nothing in this story suggests that some brash young Nigerian military officer should get up one day with the zeal of a diabolical messiah and shoot any head of state past or present before that much-endowed country can acquire the necessary discipline to enable the majority of its people to come out of the woods and realize their enormous potential. It may sound terribly out of tune with today's tendency among those entrusted with the husbandry of public resources to gorge themselves without restraint in the so-called "sharp sharp" culture.

As Governor of Judea, Nehemiah had the right to exact taxes and draw a generous allowance for himself and his entourage. Instead, the gentleman forfeited his allowance and used his own resources to support more than a hundred of his compatriots who ate at his table regularly.

Confront Evil in Public

When Nehemiah discovers that the rich Jews were enslaving their poor kinsmen through usurious loans, he acted decisively. He summoned an open town meeting and put the problem squarely on the table to demand an immediate solution. Having obtained the commitment of the noble and the rich to abandon their unjust ways, he took legal steps by ensuring that they signed an agreement witnessed by the priests. Furthermore, he sealed it with the spiritual symbolism of a conditional curse in the presence of all the assembly.

Nehemiah had the authority to summon and pronounce as the governor appointed by the emperor. However we see that in this instance, he confronted the evil not so much with the extension of the imperial authority that he carried. He rather used moral appeal and called on the legal and spiritual authority of the priests to seal the agreement.

Evil prefers to thrive in darkness. When it is exposed to the light of day, it finds it difficult to stand the scrutiny.

But what happens when the minority that has the money and power has entrenched vested interests in the anomalies and iniquities that prevail in the land?

Delegate on Merit

In the 13th chapter of the cup-bearer's memoirs, we see him appointing treasurers over the storehouses. There is testimony about the men appointed to these responsible positions in the province. They were counted faithful. There is no indication that Nehemiah used any other criterion other than this testimony of faithfulness that constituted merit for a job that required integrity and fairness in the treatment of virtually everybody.

THE BATTLES WITHIN

We have examined the nature and the tactics of the Horonite and to what extent he will go to stop you, compromise you or change your agenda. We have looked at some of the strategies that you can use to counter him and focus on your great and good work. That is not the end of the story. While the external threats to your great and good work are real obstacles that you have to surmount, there is the need to look inside and deal with the demons within. We have already taken a look at the demon of discouragement. There are others more or less sinister.

Theology teacher and octogenarian preacher, David Jeremiah prefers to label these demons that lurk in the crevices of our subconscious mind as giants. In his insightful book on overcoming the negativities in human character, "Slaying the Giants in Your Life", he identifies 11 others in addition to discouragement that if given a chance will prey on your commitment to your great and good work. They include anger, doubt, failure, fear, guilt, jealousy, loneliness, procrastination, resentment, temptation and worry. If you can overcome this plethora of internal enemies then you will indeed be able to coast effortlessly through your great and good work. However we are human beings subject to various limitations in our abilities and capabilities. You can be sure that in your efforts to accomplish your great and good work, you will face one of these giants in one form or another every step of the way. Knowing that they are there, lurking and determined to pounce at any opportunity but absolutely unwilling to come out into the light gives you an advantage over them. Once you bring the light of consciousness to shine on them, you will find that they are not as powerful as they seem. Neither will their menacing hold on your ability to act be strong again.

The Sanballats, the Tobiahs and the Gershems will not relent from assaulting you from without but the assaults from the demons within are the more devastating in their negative impact. Their capacity to block your way, like pernicious giants, to the attainment of your great and good work must be neutralized for you to be able to proceed day to day, with commitment and determination towards the accomplishment of your great and good work. The battles to be fought are mostly within.

From Joseph to Nehemiah

There is another man of the Near East whose name has become one of the most popular in Christendom and Islamiyah put together. I am referring to good old Yusuf bin Yaqub also known as Joseph son of Jacob. Joe's brothers hated him because his father pampered him too much. To make matters worse he had this annoying habit of dreaming dreams that put him in a superior position to them. They conspired and sold him into slavery where he ended up in the house of wealthy Potiphar, the chief of staff of the Pharaoh of Egypt. Egypt of course was the country to be at that time. It was the America of several of the BC millennia. The story of how Joseph rose to become the number 2 man in the whole of Egypt is a familiar one with its own drama and lessons. That indeed is a story for another day.

Of Principled Balls and a Woman Scorned

For now however, the story of how he handled his sexuality is the one that interests us. The man must have been practically oozing sex appeal to have so captivated his master's wife that she decided to make it a do or die mission to bed the young man and sample the stuff of which he was made. And Joseph fled from the no doubt very attractive and powerful woman leaving his coat behind. Hell hath no fury like a woman scorned and Lady Potiphar made sure that Joseph spent time in jail for having such principled balls.

Later potentates of the near east made sure that their loyal servants had no problems with libidinous temptations. They took their balls before anyone could say "genital mutilation!" Couldn't have them contending with sexual problems that might distract their attention from full service to the king.

Not much is known of the personal and family life of Nehemiah. Commentators on his life however indicate that he was actually born in exile and must have been well educated in the ways of the Persian Empire and royalty to have risen to the highly confidential position of cup-bearer to the "king of kings" Artaxerxes.

No reference is made to Nehemiah's family in his memoirs and in other writings that refer to him. Some scholars say he was most likely a eunuch. It is therefore quite likely that Nehemiah had no children to inherit what he was dedicating his life to restore and preserve. To make his mark on the history of his people he had to conceive of a goal that was larger than his appetite, his family fortune and his tribe.

Nehemiah was aware that the man from whom he had to seek favor to be able to embark on his mission of reconstruction and restoration was possibly responsible for his no balls status. He had enough courage, faith and humility to go to the man while trusting God implicitly to work on the man's heart for the accomplishment of his purpose. To succeed in your great and good work, you will need to bring under total subjection the demon of pride that foists your ego on a pedestal and mesmerizes you with narcissistic self-admiration.

Libidinous Excesses

The demon of libidinous excess is the other one against which you need to be on the watch out. The French have an apt saying "Cherchez la femme" which means "Look for the woman." In all cases of conflict and anomalous relationships among men in societies, the root cause is likely to have something to do with a woman. Quite often, the recto verso also applies. When I delve into the roots of my Tiv cultural milieu and the social history of this fiercely exogamous community, I am amazed at the reality of the French saying.

There is nothing this side of eternity that conveys a man to the gates of heaven or dashes him to the depths of hellish despair as the primordial emotion associated with the libido. No wonder, a sane and reasonable man can become a beast when the sexual urge or any of its derivatives manifests with power under the right or wrong circumstances. And so it was with the first Tiv man to be incarcerated in the White man's prison in the early days of the British colonial rule in Tivland.

Our character was a wealthy and respected man among his peers. Of course one of the marks of status in society at the time was the number of wives in one's harem and he had a goodly number spread across a broad age spectrum. One of the first Tiv men to go to the white man's prison did so for inserting his rather robust manhood in his young wife's ear and jamming it in rather forcefully to drive home his point. Since she chose not to use those auditory appendages for listening to his message of fidelity to him alone, perhaps she would rather respond to the sensation in her ear.

Of course the white man did not agree and he had to serve a term in his jail for a crime against humanity.

The inter-clan wars fought among the various clans of Tiv also invariably traced their origins to conflicts over exchange marriages gone awry or elopements not approved by the relatives of the would-be bride. The exchange marriage was in times gone by a reciprocal means of assuring stability in marriage among contracting families and clans. The union was an ever-lasting bond that could not be lightly broken. As a male of marriageable age, you needed a sister or a female relative who stood in place of a blood sister to be able to initiate an exchange marriage.

Armed with your "sister" allocated by the elders of the extended family with the right to share the female members for the purpose of exchange marriage, you went out to hunt for a suitable partner from an exogamous clan. Once you had identified your target, you found out who her "brother" was. If your discreet enquiries indicated that the family in question was good stock and held the possibility of a positive trade, you then made the approach.

"I have seen a ripe and juicy mango in your orchard that my heart desires to pluck," you might broach the subject with your prospective brother-in-law.

"Really?" he might ask. "And what would you have to offer in exchange for mango?"

"A ripe yellow orange that I am sure your heart will pant after. Would you like to come and see?"

The brothers would then arrange for the other prospects to meet and size up each other. If the prospective bridegrooms agreed, in principle, further steps would be taken to formalize the approach and go through the processes that would cement the union between the contracting families and clans. The end result was simple. You marry my sister and I marry your sister. We are reciprocal in-laws.

But there are some complications. You are responsible for your sister's welfare in my home just as I am responsible for my sister's welfare in your home. We are in short, the protectors and guardians of our sisters. If your sister gets sick, I can send her back to you to take care of the problem before returning her to me. In the meantime, I can withdraw my sister to carry out the duties of your sister with the exception of the bedroom ones. If your sister is fertile and has six children with me while my sister only managed two, you could come and take two of my children so that we could balance up with four children each. The tensions and conflicts that could result from this extended family arithmetic as well as the tangled web of intricate relationships could lead to outright war among the Tiv clans.

In more recent history, the conflict between Chief J. S. Tarkaa and the indomitable Godwin Akpenlamen Dabo, both of blessed memory is believed to have been sparked by competition over a woman. Alhaji Babatunde Jose, the Baba of the journalism profession in Nigeria aptly captured it in a cartoon idea that was beautifully interpreted by Josy Ajiboye, "If you Tarka me, I will Daboh you."

YOU ALREADY MESSED WITH ME MISTER

As the succeeding generations of leaders in our continent and elsewhere become younger and brasher in their demeanor, the problems of libidinous excesses are bound to increase. Accurate are the words of the sage who said that power is the most potent aphrodisiac. Of course if the owners of the libido, like Joseph are prepared to harness it with discipline, then the only woman that needs to be found is the one behind her husband's success. The demon of libido and all that it entails and spawns need to be brought under control if one is to succeed in channeling his or her energies to the realization of his or her great and good work.

Don't Break My Colt's Back

In an adaptation of Aesop's fables, the story is told of a man who had an extensive paddy of rice that was growing green and strong on the banks of the Donga River. One evening, as he strolled through the rice farm with his kid brother, he started to day-dream.

"One day," he said, "when I harvest this rice and sell it, I will get plenty of money. I will buy a horse, a real mighty beast, all black. And when I sit on its back all bedecked in the anger cloth of deepest black and white stripes, I will sing with the loudest voice as I ride from Tor Donga to Anyiin boasting to my age-mates: 'Among all of you, who is like me?' Won't that be marvelous kid brother?"

"Wonderful!" retorted kid brother with enthusiasm, "and when your horse has a colt, I will ride that colt and ride it and ride it."

Immediately, big brother grabbed little brother and started giving him the thrashing of his life. A passer-by asked him why he was beating his kid brother so mercilessly.

"He is trying to break my colt's back!" he retorted angrily. The passer-by moved on quickly fearing as Africans are wont to do very quickly, that he may have dropped into some surreal world.

If we avoid the "Don't break my colt's back" syndrome, then we will not count our chickens before they are hatched but nurture every chicken and every egg to ensure maximum hatch. At the base of this syndrome are the twin demons of jealousy and greed. They have to be eschewed from within and excluded from without.

In my years of interacting with African institutions and personalities, I find this syndrome manifesting so often to the detriment of so many good initiatives that I think it deserves serious consideration by anyone who seriously aspires to the accomplishment of any great and good work.

The East African Community predated the European Community by several decades. The East African Community had a common currency, common services, and a common passport and tariff regime through out the countries of Kenya, Tanzania and Uganda. There was free movement of goods and labor, and the parliament of the East African community was vibrant and effective. The economic structure was organized to give each component the opportunity to exercise and optimize the effectiveness of its area of competitive advantage. It all came crashing down a few years after independence. Perceptions of grandeur and real or imagined hurts set what would have been the pioneer regional economic and political block years behind its potential. We hope that the renewed efforts to resuscitate and consolidate this pioneer regional cooperation block and others like it will not flounder on the altar of an imaginary broken colt's back.

Please Don't Milk the Foetus

A variant of the colt's back syndrome is the milking of the fetus. This a tendency to greedily grab for benefits from perceived or assumed largesse before projects have had a chance to gestate and begin to yield profit or results of any kind.

It has become a practice widely accepted in the public services of many African states that contracts awarded have to be loaded up with spurious expenses and skimmed from the top before any work is done. Others have gone so far as to not only skim but scrape a large chunk of flesh from the body proper of resources designated for the project. This accounts for the plethora of uncompleted projects that dot the African landscape, particularly in countries like my fatherland Nigeria where the pattern seems to have been set in the early years of the oil boom. However, it would appear that with each succeeding generation of leaders, the temptation to milk the fetus grows with their gargantuan appetites.

MILKING THE FOETUS

A story that I have found popular with the inhabitants of the corridors of power from the East and West of the continent pokes fun at a couple of corrupt leaders that exchange visits and banter about their corrupt practices. The first place I heard it was at a diplomatic party in Nairobi Kenya at the time the Kenyan vice-president was having a spot of trouble with a Forex scam called Goldenberg.

In this version of the story, an African vice-president went to visit his Italian counterpart in good old Roma. The host took his guest on a tour of the ancient and modern city that ended up in his penthouse atop a glistening high rise building in the choicest part of town. The African was impressed. He asked his Italian counterpart. "I hear that real estate in this part of the city comes at something like a Million per square meter. How did you do it?"

"Easy," retorted his host. "You see that Olympic stadium where your guys are going to come in a few weeks' time to outrun everybody?" The African nodded affirmation. "Ten percent," said the Italian. After sampling more of the delights of the city of Caligula and Julius Caesar, the host took his guest to visit his extensive vineyards in the country.

"This is really marvelous. How did you do it?" the African vice-president asked with unfeigned enthusiasm. "See that new high-speed metro line you took from the airport to the Olympic village?" The African nodded once more. "Ten percent," concluded the Italian.

In due course, the Italian returned the visit and his African counterpart was only too delighted to show him his own possessions ranging from choice real estate in the capital to the impressive collection of regular and exotic animals in his ranches and game parks.

"I don't understand. Your country is poor. We give you aid to meet your basic needs. How did you make it?" "I will soon show you," the African vice-president responded somewhat mysteriously. They climbed into the chopper that would take them back to the city after a sumptuous meal of eland marinated in choice herbs and sautéed in select vegetables of the coastal Kambe washed down with Mnazi. As the chopper gained height, the African vice president pointed down to his guest. "Do you see that ten-lane causeway skirting the coastal mainland and those two bridges that link our most popular tourist islands to the causeway and the mainland?" The Italian shielded his eyes, afraid that the delicious African eland and the humid heat of the coast might have started playing a few tricks on his senses. "I see nothing" he ventured. "Exactly!" his host replied. "One hundred percent!"

The laughter that greeted this punch line spoke of the deep appreciation of the wit of the story that also embodied a tacit approval of the morality and ethical orientation of the highly-placed public officials. The story has a ring of universality about it. I have heard various versions in ball-rooms and bars across Africa usually to the raucous laughter of the elite in the corridors of power. They seem to be encouraging one another to be bold in their corruption efforts. "After all, the Italians and the Japanese, the Arabs and the Israelis are doing it. Go ahead, help yourself."

Told in less affluent circumstances, it goes to buttress the lingering suspicion of the talakawa that their leaders, whether ten-per centers or hundred per centers are doing unsavory things with their resources and their heritage.

An indication that there might be some credibility to this suspicion was recently demonstrated in the one and only Heartbeat of Africa, the giant in the sun, Nigeria, the country endowed with such a humungous resource base that no-one needs attempt the milking of a fetus. It has however carried the syndrome from the ridiculous to the sublime. The election year of 2007 in Nigeria will be remembered for its drama and its arrant manifestation of milking the fetus and the broken colt's back syndrome.

The two top gentlemen in the land had for more than a year been at each other's throats spitting venomous accusations as to who was the bigger thief or who had been more reckless with the resources of the nation and the criminal flaunting of the constitution that they had both sworn to protect. It is said that the vice president scuttled the desire of his boss to elongate his tenure with a third term, probably a first step to a presidency for life. The number two man did this in order to protect his interest. He was after the big job himself. His boss promptly decided "if you Tarka me, I Daboh you." He thereafter brought out his substantial manhood and urinated on the plans of number two. In fact he had been heard to advise political opponents: "Do anything you want as long as you don't hobnob with number two." Milking of the fetus and the breaking of the colt's back syndrome both have this ridiculous characteristic of riding with certainty into the unknown. Imagine that the cow is pregnant. It is not known whether it will put to bed a male or female. You don't know if the pregnancy will even come to term. Even if she yielded a female calf, it would have to be nurtured and get to the stage where it starts producing milk in its own right. That is when you start milking it. The guy who thrusts his hand in the cow's innards seeking to milk the fetus of course attempts to solve an equation with too many unknowns. Invariably, what he brings out and assumes to be milk is likely to be blood, like blood money. The same goes for the field of rice that is yet to seed not to mention the fact that it has to ripen, get harvested, processed and taken to the market before it can be sold to yield money for the horse that has to go through the natural processes of the birds and the bees to produce a colt.

The temptation to milk the fetus is not restricted to the high and mighty. Each employee that cares not a hoot what investment his employer has in a venture and pilfers and cuts corners to make a quick buck at the expense of the business is milking the fetus. Please don't milk the fetus.

The Akambe Shin Gber Syndrome

As a child growing up in the villages of the Benue Valley of Nigeria, one of the delights that I enjoyed along with my age-mates was hunting in the marshes for crabs and frogs. These inhabitants of the marshes in which our parents cultivated rice provided good protein supplementation for us children. Every full-blooded Tiv of our generation of course knows that waiting for meat in your regular diet could be long. There are several reasons for this. Meat was only served on special occasions. You could not for instance just wake up and kill a chicken because you feel like eating meat. Your relatives will say it is because you know your death that you have decided to destroy the livestock. You waited for an appropriate visitor to kill the chicken so that you could also have a piece for your craving.

My great grand-mother Imodeh left a legend in her Amorka sub-clan of Mbayion with her antics for satisfying her craving for meat. It does appear that the Tiv's craving for meat increases with age. So great-grandma Imodeh found a way of ensuring that she could have some chicken or goat meat when the craving hit her hard without incurring opprobrium from the clan.

Since her home was a short walk from the major East-West road that linked the Eastern and Southern clans of the tribe to their northern and western kith and kin, she would take the short walk and wait. If she saw a decent-looking person passing, she would approach him and begin to question him on his lineage. Since all the Tiv are supposed to have descended from one progenitor, you can always find a close enough blood relationship with any other Tiv person if you search hard enough. Imodeh would by careful questioning find just that relationship, and voila, a chicken has to die to celebrate reconnection with this long-lost relative.

"Come and visit me," she would expansively invite the stranger. "Come and visit me so that I can kill a chicken for you and also satisfy my craving," the latter statement uttered sotto voce.

You can understand that in a society where killing a chicken had to go through such desperate protocol, the palates of children would not rate very high on the distribution schedule when it came to sharing the meat of the chicken or whatever animal happened to go under the knife for the special occasion. In fact, the children would generally get the talons, the head or the neck of the chicken as standard fare. Hunting for crab and frog in the marshes to supplement our protein needs was a good pass time and a fun game.

The crab by the way is a tidy animal with a high degree of environmental awareness. When she digs her hole in the marshes, she cements it nicely and clears the entrance of all debris. The water in the crab hole is generally clean and clear. Being also jealous of its territory, it dashes out to check any intrusion. And that is how we usually got it. We would put a stick or an adventurous hand in the crab hole and muddy the water. The crab would dash out angrily to check who was disturbing its peace. We would scoop it up before it had recovered its composure and drop it in the gourd that we carried for that purpose. A gourd by the way is a calabash with a narrow neck. Once the crab passed the neck and dropped in the belly of the gourd, it became extremely difficult for it come out. If we wanted to amuse ourselves further with the helpless crabs in the gourd, we would drop a piece of yam or potato in the gourd and you would hear the crabs scratching and jostling inside and creating a right royal shindig as they struggled over the morsel in the gourd.

Some people tend to see the world in terms of the gourd. Once they find themselves in an organization, it is as if that institution has become the whole universe. They will kick and scratch and pull and push every other person in their way in pursuit of their interests. While the poor crab was separated from his home in the marshy expanse, imprisoned in the gourd with others of its type and forced into competition for morsels, human beings always have alternatives and do not have to be trapped or strangulated by the *akambe shin gber (*crabs in the gourd) syndrome. In choosing your great and good work, the whole world is out there to be explored, researched, subjugated and dominated. You do not have to be caught up in the *akambe shin gber* syndrome.

The Demons Galore Syndrome

The rise and rise of some Pentecostal denominations in the proliferation of churches across the land and the enculturation of the great religions in some African communities has given rise to a new plethora of demons. There is what some have called the reintroduction of witchcraft into the Church through the back door. In some of these congregations, the emphasis has shifted dramatically from the good news of the accomplished work of God in His creation to the terrible news of the Devil and His agents waiting to finish you around every bend that you take and every space in which you pass. The terrible news goes further. The Devil has agents in your family. They are your close relatives who are in close collaboration with their master casting spells to ruin you, kill you and your children for no justifiable cause whatsoever. Can't you see how their activities are working against your progress and your good wherever you are. By the power of their witchcraft, they can transcend space and time to reach you and yours wherever you are and do you harm.

Don't bring your children near them if you want them to live into healthy adulthood. The corollary is obvious. You should be suspicious of your relatives. In fact, you should hate them for all the evil spells they have been casting on you and yours. And when you get down on your knees to pray, or better still, stand in battle array as you storm the gates of heaven with your powerful prayers, do not forget to call down fire and brimstone on their heads and ask God to destroy them *kpatakpata*. And while you are at it, don't forget to heap a generous helping of insults on their master the Devil and all his demons from the pit of hell!

Through the demons galore syndrome, the religion of Christianity, based on love is being rapidly changed by the spurious hate-filled doctrines of these pernicious denominations into one of irrational suspicion and hatred. It should be instructive that the antics of some of these denominations are not found in the Bible or any holy book.

Of course, if your relationship with members of your family is tainted by suspicions of witchcraft and demonic activity at every turn, how will you ever come together to think collectively and pull together in a positive effort to accomplish some great and good work?

For those who desire to dwell in the shadow of perpetual obscurity and consign their people to the dustbin of development, there could be no better master stroke than the adoption and promotion of the demons galore syndrome.

This syndrome is steeped in the fear of death. It arrogates to man the power of God and the Devil put together and by planting the seeds of discord, suspicion, fear and hatred in the family. It subverts the family that was created as the primary school of love and the channel for the receipt and distribution of God's blessings to mankind.

To overcome the crippling consequences of the demons galore syndrome, you must first overcome the fear of death even as Nehemiah and the other models we have examined did. You must enthrone love instead of hatred and suspicion in your dealings relating to your great and good work. The great religions attribute the responsibility for revenge to God and leave it at that.

When you are consumed with your great and good work and those who are steeped in mean and petty machinations try to hurt you, you can afford to say with the Master Jesus when they were driving nails through his hands: "Father forgive them for they know not what they do."

CHOOSING YOUR GREAT
AND GOOD WORK

Nehemiah based his choice of a great and good work on what he had found out about the situation of his people back in Jerusalem. He was able to clearly articulate his request to Emperor Artaxexes.

"How can I not be sad? For the city where my ancestors are buried is in ruins and the gates have been burned down.' 'Well, what should be done?' the king asked. With a quick prayer to the God of heaven, I replied, 'If it please Your Majesty and if you look upon me with your royal favor, send me to Judah to rebuild the city of my fathers."

Although Nehemiah had gone into depression at the contemplation of the situation of his beloved Jerusalem, when the call came to think and to act, he was able to see the potential that lay on the other side of the problem. This perception is embodied in the second part of his request to the emperor.

'If it please the king, give me letters to the governors west of the Euphrates River instructing them to let me travel through their countries on my way to Judah; also a letter to Asaph, the manager of the king's forest, instructing him to give me timber for the beams and for the gates of the fortress near the temple, and for the city walls and for a house for myself.' And the king granted these requests for God was being gracious to me."

Nehemiah was conscious of the resources that were available for the accomplishment of his great and good work and had the foresight to obtain the necessary permission and empowerment from the emperor to be able to access them for the work.

When we look at the problems of Africa or sometimes just those of our nation, state, local government or community, they can appear so formidable that we may fail to look on the other side to see the resources and the opportunities that they present for the accomplishment of not just one but a myriad of great and good works.

Building Walls and Breaking Walls

In confronting our realities and the challenges they pose to our beloved city of our fathers whatever it may be; we will probably find that we have to break down as many walls as we are building others up. We need to build the walls that will protect the values that we hold dear for the health and positive development of our families, communities, nations and societies at large. We will need to break down the walls of hatred, selfishness, greed and moral decadence that threaten the health and well-being of our lands and people beginning with the most fundamental of the building blocks of society, the family.

The Family

In a time when the foundation of society is buffeted by many contradictory forces and ideologies, the family is the most logical place to start. For those who believe, the family is God's creation and it is the most fundamental and important organizational unit of mankind. The scientific basis of the family is of course based on the fact that members of the same family share the genetic code that endows them with certain physical characteristics that differentiate them from others. For everyone, the family is the most important human institution for the transmission of values, the sustenance of enduring traditions and contribution to the evolution of culture. It is the building block of the larger society to which we can all contribute.

Train up a Child

"Train up a child in the way he should go; even when he is old, he will not depart from it." This is an often quoted saying that is taken from the Proverbs of Solomon and is used liberally in discussions about family. Training in childhood has a lasting impact throughout a human beings lifetime. Most people who use the quotation however are not aware of the fact that the person who gave this exhortation that has been proved true through the ages also had an elaborate curriculum for the training which follows hard on the heels of the exhortation. And the curriculum is paraphrased as follows:

1. Work hard and establish your independence so that you will not fall under the control of your lenders
2. Don't be unjust in your dealings or you will fall into serious trouble
3. Be generous with your substance and you will be blessed
4. Don't be quarrelsome or abusive or associate with quarrelsome and abusive people
5. Be pure in heart and gracious in your speech so that you will have positive influence in high places
6. Keep to the truth and God will vindicate you

7. Don't be lazy and find ridiculous excuses for failing to do what you should
8. Avoid the trap of sexual immorality for it kindles God's anger
9. Give and take punishment for silly and careless behavior
10. Don't give bribes to the rich or oppress the poor to get rich or you will become poor yourself.

These ten exhortations for virtuous living are followed by 30 wise sayings that summarize the main ethical, relational and practical issues of living. These ethical principles, if internalized will make it extremely difficult for their practitioner to become wayward or negative in his or her orientation.

I recently had occasion to ask an elder statesman of Nigeria what he thought is the greatest challenge of leadership in Nigeria today. He answered without hesitation. "Whoever can help us to restore the ethical foundations of our society today would have accomplished the greatest leadership achievement of our times." The ethical foundations of our society are laid with the cultivation of values that are taught in the family. As a member of a family with a leadership role to play in the cultivation of the values that form the ethical foundation of our society, you certainly have a great and good work that you can embark on, in the family.

If every mum and Dad, every uncle and aunty, big brother and big sister chose to internalize these values of the Solomon curriculum and impart them to the younger generations in their families, we would no doubt be on the way to the realization of the ethical foundation that our elder statesman craves along with millions of other Nigerians and Africans.

Community

Most of the people in my generation grew up in villages with a strong sense of community. If you happened to be the literate one in the village where the majority could barely read or write, your rare talents were available to the village at large for carrying out those chores that needed their application; like writing and reading letters. You might be playing football with your pals, where football consisted of an inflated pig's or bull's bladder wrapped up in in rags for body mass, when you heard your mum's clear sonorous voice calling your name. Atsen! Atseneou! I suppose the suffix . . . eou was meant to emphasize something like "It's me your mother calling. Better leave whatever you are doing and come here immediately." Obediently you abandon your play after a last-ditch effort at getting the bladder in swaddling clothes through the improvised goalpost of two small mounds of stones as you responded for good measure, "Mama, I am coming ooo!". As you ran towards the mango tree in front of Mama's house, you saw Mama Kahemban whose children were scattered in various distant cities and towns of Nigeria as part of the Tiv Diaspora sitting on a stool. If there was a plain sheet of paper folded over and stuck neatly in the crack of a serrated reed, you knew there was a letter to be written to one of her children. If there was an envelope stuck in the reed, you knew there was a letter to read.

Mama Kahemban's husband could read in the Tiv language. After all, he was one of the early teachers to graduate from the vernacular teachers' classes organized by the missionaries of the Dutch Reformed Church Mission when they ventured from the wine groves and orange orchards of the Western Cape to Tivland in Central Nigeria in first quarter of the 20ᵗʰ century. He could not read his sons' letters though because they were written in English. I suppose the children had to show that they had arrived by writing to their parents in the white man's language. So Atsen had to be called in.

Mama Kahemban smiles revealing the gap in the middle of the upper row of snow-white teeth, enhanced by the black and pink of her gums. You like her and her strapping sons, both the one who was in the army and the one who worked for the railways as a linesman. You lean against the wall of your mother's house and read the letter in English sentence by sentence and interpreted it in Tiv to Mama Kahemban who certainly knew the way to a child's heart. She knew that you liked the aromatic brown bean pudding especially when it was cooked in a generous red palm oil sauce spiced with a touch of *tatashe* peppers and a nice sprinkling of *yiye* spice. She has kept a generous loaf of your favorite which she gives you at the end of the reading and interpretation. You enjoy the delicacy with relish and wash it down with cold water from your mother's osmotic cooler earthen pot before you go gamboling back to your game with the boys. In the village, you knew everybody and almost everybody knew you.

The growth of urbanization in most countries of the world has reduced to a great extent the ties that one felt through kinship in a close-knit village environment and eroded the sense of community. But who says this is not an opportunity for a great and good work? Is there not an opportunity for a great and good work in creating communities in the concrete jungles where people are dying of loneliness in crowded cities and towns? A great and good work can be found in creating communities united around positive goals and projects in today's lonely concrete jungles. Other great and good works can be found in the role of reader interpreter among the marginalized and disconnected from the media and local government in the urban slums or the rural hinterland.

Natural Resources

If the continent of Africa were to effectively harness and equitably and optimally exploit even 10% of its resource potential, its nations would have no business exporting economic refugees to any other region of the world.

With 40% of the world's potential hydro-electric power supply, 50% of gold, 90% of cobalt, 40% of platinum, 64% of manganese, and vast amounts of diverse mineral, plant and animal resources, Africa would seem to be endowed with all the natural resources required for the attainment of economic greatness. But the reality is steeped in paradoxes.

Nigeria has more than 110 trillion standard cubic feet of gas reserves and about 10 trillion cubic feet of oil reserves, a production output capacity of more than 2 million barrels of crude a day and climbing. The country was however more than $50 billion dollars in debt and sliding farther and farther down the ladder of the poor highly indebted and corrupt countries of the globe until a retired General who was pulled from prison and elevated to the Presidency of the land decided to take the bull by the horns and negotiate a deal to end the indebtedness. Noises and sounds coming out of the economic woodwork indicate that as these things go, Nigeria may still be very far from coming out of the woods as far as debt is concerned.

Apart from the humungous figures that defy rational analysis at the level of the average African, there are always the complications of international high finance triple-speak mediated by the Bretton Woods sisters. Talking about the trillions of cubic metres of incendiary detritus for many Nigerians evokes memories of their compatriots burnt to cinder in valiant fatal attempts to scoop fuel from punctured pipelines or overturned oil tankers. Identifying that microcosmic level where you and I can play, how does the natural resources route provide opportunity for the choice and realization of a great and good work?

Natural resources can be conserved, developed, multiplied, exploited and optimized at the micro and macro levels. Take water for instance.

Forty years since we drew the lines in the sands of Akpagher market to trade grandiloquence in "Shon" competitions, I was moved by the spirit to go visiting that village in which I had coined my first poetic words and began to develop an awareness of the society around me. I went in on Easter morning to worship at the church of NKST Kuhe, one of those that my father had helped to plant in his Evangelising days. The congregation received me with joy and I was happy to see some of the old women still recognized me and called me by my pet name of "Aticha". Aticha, plural for teacher in the Tiv language stuck fast to me in my pre-teen years. Once a month, all the teachers from the various Christian Religious Instruction (CRI) classes scattered throughout Mbatiav clan used to converge at Kuhe for a three-day meeting. I had a knack for giving onomatopoeic responses that were supposed to illustrate in one word, the characters of the teachers from any particular location present at the meeting. It was usual to find me during these three days surrounded by adults and children alike egging me on to describe the teachers from one school or another. I never missed a beat and for some reason, my coinages left both adults and children in stitches. I was happy to be so remembered and I spent a good morning and afternoon with some of the families. I also recalled the saying all those years ago that there were two ways of having your bath in Akpagher. You could run your selected course and work up a heavy sweat and then use a reed to scrape off the sweat from your body. Alternatively, you could use one grain measure popularly known as the mudu in Hausa with a piece of cloth to rub the water in it on your skin. So scarce was water in Akpagher.

I was shocked to find out that more than forty years down the road, this community had never found a Nehemiah who could mobilize it and say: "Let us dig a well or build a dam that will provide water for our needs and rid us of this perpetual curse." I was shocked to find that the young women and men in two of the families that I visited had left early in the morning to go for water at a well that took them more than half a day to reach and return. Will Akpagher ever find a Nehemiah who can mobilize the people to solve their water problem?

The Taste of Shibila and Alakpa

I enjoyed the dry season in the villages of the Benue Valley. It was the season that brought forth the mature yam in its glory and the seed yams in their tantalizing shapes and sizes. As a kid running around naked around my mother's yam farm, I could identify by name and distinct characteristic more than 12 species of yam. I understand at that time, there were actually about 32 species being actively grown and propagated throughout the farms in Tivland. My favourites were Alakpa and Shibila. You roasted the slim and svelte Alakpa in fire embers, never the flame. It cooked soft and fluffy and you just peeled off the skin and dipped it in salted red palm oil if you wanted to enhance the taste any further. Shibila had this distinct amber-coloured bottom. Whether you boiled it or roasted it, first it would announce through its cooking aroma that you were in for a good time and then when you actually bit into it, the response was really good.

You may never taste Alakpa or Shibila ever again because for all I know, they could be extinct. Lack of attention to biodiversity and the selection of two or three species of yam with limited genetic characteristics but the capacity to produce huge tubers have assured the extinction of several exotic species. There is no doubt that the Creator had unique utility for each of the genetic characteristics encoded in the wide variety of species in existence before the choice of size over diversity. There are many great and good works that can be done with the conservation and development of natural resources at the family and community levels where you and I can play as individuals and groups.

However, deciding on your great and good work involves the making of choices based on your understanding of who you are, where you are, what you are and why you are.

When I set out to look at Nehemiah's model of a strategy for reconstruction, it seemed pretty clear to me that I was talking to the African Diaspora in Europe and North America. It seemed pretty clear to me that this group with the advantage of exposure to the technology of the Western World as well as its financial systems and material needed encouragement to make a positive contribution to the development of Africa. It seems to me that we may need to broaden the definitions and enable you to find your comfortable place within them, a place that will enable you to most effectively define your great and good work and effectively carry it out.

National Development

In the third quarter of the last century, a gentleman by the name of Johann Galtung came up with an analytical framework that he called his hypothesis of structural imperialism. This was later proved and accepted as theory. Galtung divided the countries of the world into centre and periphery countries. You did not have to go to great lengths to realize that the centre countries belonged to the industrialized North while the periphery countries generally belonged to the impoverished South. What I found particularly interesting about Galtung's theory was his subdivision of the internal structures of the centre and periphery countries. He held that in the centre countries, you had the centre of the centre and the periphery of the centre. The people in the centre of the centre controlled the economic and power structure of the country while the periphery was generally marginalized and powerless. In the periphery countries, there was the centre of the periphery and the periphery of the periphery. The centre of the periphery performed the same functions as the centre of the centre in the periphery countries with the periphery of the periphery equally marginalized and powerless. What was even more interesting was the fact that the linkage between the centre of the centre and the centre of the periphery was established. While the flow of information and communication between the people in the two centre groups was normal, the flow between the two periphery groups was generally distorted and full of misinformation and disinformation.

As I have reflected on the definition of the Diaspora and the various groups to which one could belong, I have been attracted again and again to Galtung's Theory. In trying to define my Diaspora pedigree, I have been confronted with the reality of foreign and domestic Diasporas. Since 1990, I have not spent more than two months at a stretch in my beloved Benue Valley in Central Nigeria until 2006/7. When I go to my village of Ahua Nduur in Mbamtegh clan of Mbayion, I meet my Makurdi Diaspora relatives, Abuja Diaspora relatives and Lagos Diaspora relatives. Then there is also the possibility of meeting my overseas Diaspora relatives.

There are perceptions and expectations of each of these Diaspora groups and one has to decide how one defines his or her Diaspora. One could stretch Galtung's Theory somewhat further and apply the concept of center and periphery within nation-states. If one took a country like Nigeria, one might find that there are center states and periphery states. In a state one might find center local governments and periphery local governments. Within local governments, one might find center communities and periphery ones.

The United Nations Development Program (UNDP) publishes the annual Human Development Report that ranks countries globally on certain common development indices. In recent years, the UN agency has conducted some social mapping studies in country that have given a more realistic picture of the wealth and poverty distribution profiles within countries as opposed to the lumped together country profile based on averaged out figures. Some of the countries of the developing world in Africa and elsewhere have also within the context of their poverty reduction strategies, come up with statistics that may present a useful picture in defining where you stand as a Diasporan in relation to the community that you define as your people.

When I lived in Kenya during the last decade of the 20ᵗʰ Century I observed that the Luo community that prides itself on sophistication and may sometimes be credited with the invention of the Angerakuzengezengezong syndrome was the butt of jokes from their compatriots. My observation was that if you met a Kenyan with a first name like Washington, Mountbatten, Pascalia, Scholatica or Euphemesia, he or she was likely to be Luo.

Anyway, Christmas and New Year season saw the brisk movement of trucks loaded with household goods ranging from chairs and mattresses to refrigerators, generators and microwave ovens heading from Nairobi and the coastal city of Mombassa to the suburbs of Kisumu and Kisauni. The Washington Odhiambos, Churchill Omondis and Pascalia Scholastica Ojangas were taking the necessities that they would use in the villages over the holiday period before carting them back into the cities where they live and work at the end of the holidays. It did not occur to them that the villagers whom they went to pass those few days with might have use of those necessities also, and perhaps if they made them a permanent feature of the villages as well as the towns, they would not have to cart them back and forth every Christmas and New Year. My Kikuyu friends who had to take only a short drive from Nairobi the capital city to their ancestral homes in the suburbs of Kiambu and Thika always had a field day poking fun at their Luo compatriots.

However with the emergence of Barrack *wuod* (son of) Obama as president of the US of A, it has deftly turned the joke on the other Kenyans especially as Kogelo, the ancestral village of the elder Obama has become a mecca of sorts. Since Kenya has refused to hand over the leadership of the country to the brilliant Luos, they have decided to export their presidential material to America. But do I say?

It is also interesting that with the devolution of power to the counties and the fact that civil servants who had become so used to

107

the Nairobi way of life that they could not possibly think of living elsewhere will now actually be living and working in the county capitals. They will have to make the ovens and the deep freezers and fridges as well as the mattresses grow in these boondoons now. So where lies your great and good work in all of this?

If we revisited with that county official with the rubbery hands in the land of *harambee* or the five-member water board in the city that refused an offer of water that was too good to refuse because of a certain sum of ten million Naira divided equally into five places, one may identify some great and good works in the area of public information. It is possible to carry out some great and good works in bringing to life provisions that exist on the statute books of nations, states and local government for the good of the people but which the people never get to learn about. Because of the advantage of enlightenment that you have through education of exposure, you could carry out great and good work in unmasking obscurantism and other negative tendencies in government at the local, state or county, and national levels and actually pave the way for the people to begin to emerge from their prisons of the mind to contribute without inhibition to governance and the development of their communities and the nation.

To Which Diaspora do you belong?

It was Nehemiah who identified with the survivals of the exile that were left in Jerusalem and those that had returned in the first wave to build the temple under Ezra. He was obviously keen on maintaining his ties with relatives in the home country and showing concern for their welfare. That was his choice. We found out when he actually engaged in his great and good work, there were Jews in the city who were no doubt rich and influential. However, we found out that they were more interested in using their advantages to impoverish and enslave their less fortunate fellow Jews until Nehemiah had to intervene to break the vicious circle that they had set up. Nehemiah narrates in his own words how he came to discover this anomaly and the steps he took to break it.

"Now the men and their wives raised a great outcry against their Jewish brothers. Some were saying, "We and our sons and daughters are numerous; in order for us to eat and stay alive, we must get grain." Others were saying, "We are mortgaging our fields, our vineyards and our homes to get grain during the famine."

Still others were saying, "We have had to borrow money to pay the king's tax on our fields and vineyards. Although we are of the same flesh and blood as our countrymen and though our sons are as good as theirs, yet we have to subject our sons and daughters to slavery. Some of our daughters have already been enslaved, but we are powerless, because our fields and our vineyards belong to others."

"When I heard their outcry and these charges, I was very angry. 7 I pondered them in my mind and then accused the nobles and officials. I told them, "You are exacting usury from your own countrymen!" So I called together a large meeting to deal with them 8 and said: "As far as possible, we have bought back our Jewish brothers who were sold to the Gentiles. Now you are selling your brothers, only for them to be sold back to us!" They kept quiet, because they could find nothing to say.

So I continued, "What you are doing is not right. Shouldn't you walk in the fear of our God to avoid the reproach of our Gentile enemies? I and my brothers and my men are also lending the people money and grain. But let the exacting of usury stop! Give back to them immediately their fields, vineyards, olive groves and houses, and also the usury you are charging them—the hundredth part of the money, grain, new wine and oil."

"We will give it back," they said. "And we will not demand anything more from them. We will do as you say."

Nehemiah could have identified with the nobles and officials and certainly would have had no problem in carving out a fief of his own in the enslavement and exploitation game. After all, he had the emperor's fiat to exert taxes and levies for the prosecution of his work. He chose to take sides with the ordinary people who were being oppressed by their privileged kith and kin. His Diaspora experience did not cause him to look down on the less fortunate of his brothers and sisters in Jerusalem.

Experience has taught us that sometimes the Diaspora experience is not even necessary for one to develop that sense of looking down one's nose at erstwhile peers in the euphoria of uncooked bellicose political power. So the story is told of these young men who with no trade or skill, no apprenticeship or tutelage except for a relationship with a powerful political godfather who wanted to rub his opponent's nose in the mud; was catapulted into political office as a local government councilor.

Now the bush rat is a high delicacy among my Tiv people of the Benue valley. Before our young politician became a councillor, he used to go rat hunting with some friends. His best friend among the hunters invited him for dinner to congratulate him on his elevation to high office. It was gratifying to note that rat hunters could also make it. The new councilor turned up in his starched blue caftan, a mark of his new status. He could hardly find a chair in his friend's house worthy of him to let himself down, starched caftan and all to sit in. He managed at last.

His friend's wife brought which consisted of pounded yam with stew made with the largest rat recently caught and smoked by her husband. The councilor looked on, unimpressed. "Do you think," he asked his friend, "that with the status I have now attained, I should still be eating rat meat?" No kudos for guessing what the friend did with his rat or for knowing that when our councilor lost his seat a few months down the road, he went hunting alone.

Your great and good work could consist of puncturing the balloons of the impostors and charlatans masquerading as officials of government against the people and showing them the light of true governance as serving.

Who are Your People?

In the three months that I have stayed consistently in Nigeria and interacted with some of the people in my beloved Benue Valley, I have come across a World Bank assisted program that is being carried out on a pilot basis in some 9 of the most rural local governments in Benue State. Known as the Local Empowerment and Environmental Management Project (LEEMP), the project has similar pilot activities in 8 other states of the Federal Republic, namely, Adamawa, Bauchi, Bayelsa, Enugu, Imo, Katsina, Niger and Oyo.

The strategy adopted in each of these pilot states is the same. In each state, some of the most rural communities are chosen. Funds jointly provided by the government of Nigeria, the International Development Association of the World Bank and the Global Environmental Facility of the United Nations are invested in activities on which the community has decided with the project management team.

According to project public information documents, the special thing about LEEMP is that "LEEMP puts rural people in the driving seat when it comes to spending public money for local development. Most of LEEMP's budget is spent directly in the rural communities on small scale projects like school blocks, boreholes, health facilities, agro-processing and cottage industries, repairing community roads, improving the environment and farming. These small scale projects are chosen by the communities themselves. The communities also manage the money and make sure that the works are done properly.

Some of the stories that the LEEMP personnel have to tell about their experiences in the most rural communities of rural Nigeria sound incredible. I have been assured by no less a personality than the LEEMP project manager in the state that they are true in 21st Century Nigeria.

Taking advantage of the dry season, LEEMP personnel hacked their way through the rain forest and emerged into one community, with the first motor vehicle ever to show itself in that environment. The first person in the community to come face to face with the iron beast, a 4x4 Nissan Patrol Jeep, was a young lady of about 17 or 18. She took off like a startled gazelle. The shock was too much for her. She had never seen such a beast in her life.

But what was even more interesting was the reaction of the political representatives of that community in the corridors of power in the state capital. The project personnel had had the foresight to take along a still camera and a video camera with which they carefully documented their initial and subsequent encounters to share with government officials and other stake holders in the state capital.

A very high state government official is reported to have called the chairman of the local government in which that community is located. "Are you sure," he asked, "that these images are from our state and in your local government?" The official could not respond. He had never had occasion to visit with that community in his tenure as local government chairman. The high state official of course had not until confronted with the images, been aware of the existence of that community as his people. So who are your people? It is possible to find them in a lost rural community, an urban slum or a college campus.

Unfortunately, in Africa, and I suspect in other developing nations of the world, some people carry the definition of "My people" to ridiculous lengths of ethno-linguistic jingoism. Their perception of their people is based more on a series of exclusions and alienations that may be responsible for defining the grounds for eventual genocide. The pernicious line of thought that takes one down this terrible route might go something like this: If you do not belong to my tribe or linguistic group, there must be something suspicious or bad about you. In fact you must have some evil design against me. You are probably just waiting for the right opportunity to harm me. I therefore have a right to be suspicious of you. In fact, I should hate you. Since you are plotting to harm me anyway, why should I wait until you actually make your harmful move? Let me do what I can to stop you.

Some political leaders therefore see their representative roles not even within the context of their constituency but in much narrower terms. A governor who for instance sees his mandate in terms of his clan and his lineage and then grudgingly his tribe and eventually his state can hardly conceive of any vision that qualifies for greatness and goodness. So who are your people?

Just as the Master Jesus responded to the question "Who is my neighbor" with the story of the Good Samaritan, your "My people" can be similarly defined as all those who need the positive contribution that you are capable and positioned to make in their lives.

Whose Cup do you bear?

Nehemiah as cup-bearer to Artaxexes had the privilege of a confidential relationship with the emperor. Fortunately, you do not have to time travel to wake up his imperial majesty to bear his cup. In the position of advantage that you now occupy, with whom or what does it bring you into confidential relations?

But maybe you need to recognize the position of privilege and advantage that you occupy before you can identify whose cup you bear and how that relationship can be translated into advocacy for your great and good work.

That you are reading this in English and following it without a problem indicates that you are ahead of some three Billion people or more in respect of this privilege. If you have a tertiary educational qualification, you are ahead of more than four billion people on this terrestrial ball in respect of this advantage. If you have a technical or artistic skill, you are ahead of more than four billion of your global compatriots. If you can pick up a local, national or international newspaper, read it and understand the editorial content as well as the advertisements and public service announcements published therein, you are ahead of more than 80% of your compatriots in respect of this privilege. In fact your access to the modern mass media of communication is akin to enjoying confidential relations with the potentates and emperors of today's global village. You can access, appreciate and utilize privileged information that is not available to the majority of your compatriots in most countries of Africa.

So whose cup do you bear in your position of privilege and advantage and how can you utilize it in advocacy for your people and their mobilization for the great and good work that you are uniquely equipped to do?

Are you prepared to choose your great and good work and to carry it out in spite of the Horonite and the Amonite and all their allies mobilized against you? Are you prepared to build in spite of the challenges of the demons within? Then let us rise up and build our families, our communities, our local governments, our states, our countries, and our continent.

The Alternative

In the book of Chronicles in the Christian Bible, the story is told of the siege of the Israeli city of Samaria by King Benhadad of Syria when there was no longer a means of sustenance for the people of the city. It is reported that one evening, the king is on a tour of his devastated city when he is accosted by a prostitute seeking justice.

"We had an agreement, my associate and I. Business is extremely bad as you know Your Majesty. Those who can get it up are not in a position to pay for our services. They don't even want them. They are on the other side of the wall baying for blood. What about our men here? They are too weak from hunger and disease to be of any use. You know Your Majesty, we have to survive. Maybe one day, this terrible nightmare will be over and we can do business again.

So we had an agreement, my associate and I. We share a room in the quarters. In fact we have shared everything since we joined the trade years ago. That's how we both got knocked up and ended up with a brat each. Well, as we have to survive and in any case we have the instruments for making the brats anyways, we agreed to eat the brats. We killed mine and had some good meals that have put new life in us up to yesterday when we had the last bit of pepper soup from its head. That was lunch yesterday. Our next meal was supposed to come from her brat starting from last night's dinner. And now horror of horrors Your Majesty! I don't know what has come over her. Not only has she denied me the food that I am entitled to, she's gone to hide her brat, I don't know where. And now I am appealing to Your Majesty, tell her to bring out her brat so that we may cook and eat. I am really running out of patience here and more than twenty-four hours of hunger pangs are not helping matters at all. Please tell her to bring out her brat that we may eat Your Majesty.

The report does not tell us how the king in his wisdom adjudicated in the matter. Perhaps we could think about how we would adjudicate if placed in such a position. "How nasty and horrible!" we may scream at this pair of callous cannibals! But if we examine our situation today, would it be far-fetched to find striking similarities to the consumption of the brats? It is indeed the grisly alternative that is presented to our getting down to the task of building.

Is there really any difference between cooking the brats and consuming their flesh and sacrificing their social, moral and spiritual development in pursuit of trinkets, bits and artifacts for our comfort from Dubai?

Is there really any difference between the baby-eating prostitutes and the men and women who in their search for wealth and power engage in horrendous occult practices that require human sacrifice? Newspaper reports in my country Nigeria give lurid accounts of the consequences that include the murder of innocent albinos and the proliferation of human baby factories whose products end up being sold like so much merchandise or worse in the concoctions of occult practitioners and their clients.

That is the alternative that stares us in the face if we refuse to rise up and break down the walls that if kept in place will destroy us and build the ones that we need to strengthen and sustain us. The cup-bearer from the court of Artaxerxes has shown us the way from across the centuries. It is time for us to rise up and build.

BEING A NEHEMIAH TODAY

Thanks to the marriage of Technology, Education and Design initiated by Richard Saul Wurman in 1984 and developed to great heights by Chris Anderson over the past 14 years, the sharing of good ideas and promotion of great and good works has become a global phenomenon. The TED Conference and the many children it has sired over the years give birth to ideas that are worth sharing every week day in cities all over the world. These conferences, talks and forums make it possible for the lamps of ideas and action to be lit and placed on platforms for the whole world to see and emulate.

There is no shortage of contemporary role models who are ordinary people motivated to do great and good things with their lives, their passions and commitments in spite of the challenges of their environments, their circumstances and the opposition of the Sanballats, The Tobiahs and the other negative and destructive forces of the day. Examples abound.

In 2007, a barely educated young man form rural Malawi, William Kamkwamba, was given the global stage to tell the world how he had built a windmill from scraps of metal sheets, wires and wood, to provide electricity to his homestead and much-needed services to his community. I have learnt about Richard Turere, a 13-year0ld Maasai boy who was worried about the loss of his community's livestock to Lions and decided to do something about it. He designed and constructed a lighting device that kept the lions away from the cattle pens at night when they would normally have attacked.

I have come across the story of 88+-year-old grandmother Doris Haddock who set out in 1999 to walk from Los Angeles to Washington to protest against the influence of money in politics and the corruption that it spawns. She arrived 18 months later at the age of 90 and has sparked a nation-wide movement in the United States for the sanitization of politics through campaign finance reform. The movement is alive and gathering momentum fifteen years after the grandmother set out alone with a sign on her chest to take her first step of the walk of more than 2,300 kilometers to start a great and good work.

I have been inspired by Jacqueline Novogratz who set out as a young woman with a backpack and a guitar with idealism in her heart and naivety in her head to change the world and has succeeded. Through thick and thin and the humility to learn from her errors and even those looked down upon by society, she has set up one of the most successful models of entrepreneurship and philanthropy in a workable combination that is making a positive impact on people's lives across the world. I have been inspired by May El-Khalil, a marathon runner who was hit by a bus while training, spent two years in hospital and underwent thirty-six surgeries to be able to walk. She could never run the marathon again but has established the Beirut Marathon, the one day in the year when the people of strife and war torn Lebanon come together with runners from all over the world to run for peace. It has continued to expand its influence in the region and around the world for peace and development.

I am inspired by Hugh Herr, the MIT scientist who lost both legs in a climbing accident some thirty years ago. He has converted this tragic event of his life into the most fulfilling career of building bionic limbs that empower the no longer disabled to perform at their peak through his expertise in robotic prosthetics.

I am inspired by Manu Prakash and his team that has created a 50-cent microscope that folds like origami and has committed himself to bringing radical new technology to global health.

I know that there is a great and good work within you that is pushing to come out. There is a wall for the protection of that which is valuable and good to you that has been broken and the gates of your community that have been burned with fire. I know that your conscience has not been seared with a hot iron and that the brokenness of your community gives you sleepless nights and forces a sad countenance on your face before the king whose cup you bear.

It is time speak the truth about the broken walls and burnt gates. It is time to get up and build. And now that you know that you can be the Nehemiah of today, speak the truth, say the prayer and get up and build.

Purpose

The purpose of this book is to provoke and stimulate you to identify and set about the great good work that cries inside you to be unleashed on your Jerusalem wall. If you want to be a Nehemiah in your environment, join in the task. Send an email to atsen.ahua@gmail.com. In the subject line indicate Nehemiah Society. Your message should be simply: I opt in.

Shon Competition, Mwalimu Julius Nyerere, Nelson Mandela, Rawlings and Generals by Dan Nyikwagh.
Grabiosis, You Messed Mister and Milking the Foetus by Joe Awuhe.

AUTHOR'S NOTE

I have used some parables and proverbs as well as true stories to highlight points in the cupbearer's strategy. Except where specifically stated, the names in the stories are fictitious and the narrative may in some cases be embelished for effect. No offense to anyone living or deceased is intended.